HIDDEN GIRLS

A Birth Mother's Story of Reunion and Reckoning

Julia MacDonnell

ISBN: 979-8-35095-667-2

eBook ISBN 979-8-35095-668-9

Other Books by Julia MacDonnell

The Topography of Hidden Stories

Fomite Press, 2021

Mimi Malloy, At Last!

Picador, 2014

A Year of Favor

William Morrow, 1995

Silence can be a plan
rigorously executed

the blueprint to a life

It is a presence
it has a history a form

Do not confuse it
with any kind of absence

Adrienne Rich, **Cartographies of Silence**

How do we move toward wholeness? How do we do right by the wronged people of the past without physical evidence of their suffering? How do we direct our record keeping toward justice?

Carmen Maria Machado, **In the Dream House**

For my children and my grandchildren

Contents

PART ONE 1

The Past Breaks In 3

The Vow Of Silence 13

Learning Curve 18

PART TWO 22

The Republic Of Shame 23

The Story Behind The Story 31

What We Carried 34

Red Lights and Erring Girls 38

Transubstantiation 43

Stories, Lost In Transit 48

Upside Down House 54

Something's Happening Here 60

Leaving Home 62

It's All Over Now 64

Desolation Row 69

The Summer That Came Before 73

Baby Daddy 75

Spinning Round And Round 77

PART THREE 81

Choose Oblivion 82

Me In My Body 89

Mother Love 93

Ghost Mother 97

Mothers Freed At Last 100

Threatened 103

Bastards/Blue Ribbon Babies 106

Best Interests 115

PART FOUR 116

Home Stretch 117

Delivery Day 120

Broken Promise 123

Surrender 125

Too Soon 128

PART FIVE 129

Silence Is A Plan 130

Bad Dreams 131

Acquiescense 132

Searching Back Then 134

Works Of Mercy 136

Remedies 140

Golden Fairy Tale 143

Reality Bites 145

Sweet Fantasies 147

Reunion Redux 148

Are You My Mother? 155

Passages 159

What's Done Is Never Done 161

Cultural Kerfuffle 168

Whoomp! There It Is! 174

Coda 179

Acknowledgements 181

About the Author 182

Selected Bibliography 183

Recommended Readings 185

PART ONE

The Past Breaks In

One winter morning about ten years ago, a mug of coffee within reach, I opened my laptop and scanned through my email, looking the way I always did for the ones I could delete and those demanding immediate attention. My desk was actually my daughter's desk from high school, in the home I'd owned for many years, a small rancher in a southern New Jersey suburb of Philadelphia. My office was still my daughter's bedroom even though she was well launched, living and working in Manhattan.

One subject line caught my eye and then my breath: Angus John MacDonnell. The world around me lurched and tilted. Angus John MacDonnell. What I'd named my first child, the son I'd surrendered to adoption soon after I turned 19 and wasn't married. Whose birth and loss forever changed the trajectory of my life. My secret son, the son I'd grieved and loved and longed to know for almost half a century. Angus John MacDonnell. A name never spoken again by anyone I knew, except once by me to my husband.

Ms. MacDonnell,

My name is ███████████████ but I was born Angus John MacDonnell on January 3rd 1967 to one Julia MacDonnell then living at 94 Pleasant St, Plainville, MA and born in Island Falls, ME. Having googled "julia macdonnell, island falls, maine" and found your website which says that your father's name was John and his father's name Angus I suspect I have found the correct person. I do not in any way wish to intrude upon you and your life other than to say thank you for having me in the first place. I am doing well and my adoptive parents, ███████████████ took very good care of me. I would love to hear from you at least to confirm you are my birth mother but again your life is your own. Please feel free to contact me or not.

Respectfully,

██████████████

Attached to this email was a photocopy of a photocopy of a document, "Non-Certified Copy of Record of Birth Prior to Adoption." Up until that moment, I believed my surrendered son's original birth record had been sealed forever by the courts in Suffolk County, Massachusetts, the county of his birth. Catholic Charities had made that promise to my family and me half a century before when they brokered his adoption: all records pertaining to it would be off limits to everyone forever. It would be as if his birth and adoption had never happened, a secret essential to my mother and father, one they maintained for the rest of their lives. (What had happened had not happened.) And yet, there it was on my laptop screen, a bedraggled photocopy of my secret first child's birth record.

I had no idea that Massachusetts had, in 2008, opened its sealed birth records to adult adoptees born before 1974. Birth parents were not informed. Nor did I know that this stunning change in adoption law happened after a long and bitter legal battle pitting adult adoptees against adoptive parents, adoption providers, and the religious organizations that sought to keep such records sealed.

The copy of my son's non-certified pre-adoption birth record, his first birth certificate, glimmered on the screen in shades of gray. It connected my current life as a university professor, published novelist, and mother of three, to the troubled teenager I'd been. Scapegoated, hidden, unable to escape the winding cloths of shame and guilt.

The document was blurred by reproduction, its travels through cyberspace, and the decades it had spent in a vault somewhere in Massachusetts. I printed it and held it in my shaking hands, a piece of paper that confirmed the facts of my lost history: the man reaching out to me was my first son, the one I'd relinquished to closed adoption when I was still a teenager. This stunning reconnection was a moment I'd always longed for but hadn't dared to hope for. It would, I believed, provide the missing piece to the unsolved puzzle at the very heart of my life.

I read and reread the document on my screen, the first time I'd seen documentary evidence of my having given up a child to adoption. I was thrilled but also dizzied, spinning backward to my nearly lifelong secret. In my euphoria, I had no idea that I was heading into danger. *Thank you for having me.* I had no idea that reunion in adoption is shattering; that it often shoves an unprepared first mother (me) back into the skin of the terrified girl she'd been when she got pregnant, a girl without resources who paid dearly, and continued to pay, for her transgressions. The last time I'd seen my baby, named for my loved paternal grandfather, he was sweet and warm and wrapped in a soft baby blanket. Then my caseworker took him from my arms and disappeared with him into a hospital elevator. Boom. Gone. Just like that. I had no hope of ever seeing him again.

Minutes after opening my son's email, I called the cell phone number he included. He answered on the first ring, as if he had been waiting. His was a booming voice, a resonant tenor like my father's and my brothers'. The sound rippled through me: a MacDonnell voice from a man who was no longer a MacDonnell. The tilted world began to spin. I tried to slow my pounding heart, to breathe steadily and deeply, to listen. We kept it superficial, safe, sharing facts. The area code of his cell phone number indicated Boston, where he was born, but he hadn't lived there since before his adoption was finalized. He couldn't quite explain why he used that area code for his cell phone, perhaps as a connection, however insignificant, to the place of his birth. Rather than in the Boston area, as I'd always believed, he'd grown up in the suburbs of Washington D.C. His new father, a lawyer, had served as general counsel, occupying the C-suite, of a major American conglomerate.

Other facts tumbled out, faster than I could absorb them. My son, himself in middle age, was a divorced IT specialist for a national restaurant chain. He lived in a major southern city. He did not have children. He was a combat veteran, a marine who'd survived two deployments during the Gulf Wars. He was the third of four adopted children. He'd grown up in a religious Irish Catholic family, one able to provide him with comforts, even luxuries: lovely homes, sleepaway camps, splendid family vacations. (I recalled my caseworker's glee as she described his family to me: a perfect ethnic and religious match! They'd even matched hair and eye color! And my own wild jealousy that I could not, as she reminded me over and over again, provide such things for him.)

Rambunctious, rebellious by his own description, he'd flunked out of two colleges before joining the military. (Just as, unbeknownst to him, his biological father had, heading off to Vietnam, never looking back, at least not at me.) After leaving the military, my son put himself through college on the GI Bill, and embarked upon his own corporate career.

We made a plan to have lunch in Philadelphia the next time he was in town for business. Waiting those weeks, I toggled between happiness, anxiety, curiosity and disquiet. I made my excruciating revelation to my other children, among the most difficult conversations I have ever had. They accepted the existence of their older half brother with more love and equanimity than I'd believed was possible.

After that, a vision of happy family took root and shimmered in my imagination: all of us together at the Thanksgiving table or hanging out together at the Jersey Shore, scorching ourselves in the sun, leaping in the waves. In my fantasies, my first son became a vital part of my family, a new addition, albeit fully grown. I'd be able to put the devastation of his surrender behind me, and heal from the deceptions that had been imposed upon me when I was too young and fragile to fight back, or to understand their lifelong consequences.

When the day came for us to meet I was nervous and as giddy as if being spun in an unstoppable revolving door. Who would he be? Would we like each other? Would he look like me?

It was a quick drive from my Camden County, N.J., home over the Ben Franklin Bridge and into Philadelphia and Penn's Landing, our designated meeting place. I was a wreck, but I managed to park and get out. It was a cold but sunny early spring day. I recognized him right away, among the nearby urban throngs: big and hearty and white-haired, my son! He was crossing a vast parking lot, the Delaware River on one side and Penn's Landings' shops and restaurants on the other. My breath caught. He was no longer that swaddled newborn I'd handed off to the caseworker. He was a big man, with a big voice! He wore glasses and was prematurely white-haired, as his namesake had been! We hugged, the first time we'd touched in 50 years. We walked to a nearby Mexican restaurant. We stumbled through our lunch. Between us on that small Formica table, with its caddy of ketchup and Cholula hot sauce, an unexpected canyon gaped open between us. Like so many men in my family, my son was garrulous, and, I thought, accustomed to being the smartest guy in the room. Even so, I sensed a layer of something else beneath his bright surface. Nothing seemed quite real.

We reached as best we could across the canyon, but had trouble moving our conversation forward. It kept stalling out. I don't remember what we said. I was overwhelmed. We must have talked about our jobs and our families, a safe conversation that tiptoed around the big hole between us, the life we had not shared though we were mother and son. I didn't feel that instantaneous genetic connection, the one I'd read about so often in reunion stories, the one I'd been hoping for. (Later I'd learn of my mistake: very few in mother/child reunions ever feel that vaunted genetic connection.) Instead I felt as if I were auditioning for a role I didn't understand and might not be right for. Maybe he felt that way too.

It turned out we both liked food, an unsurprising discovery, but one that helped ease the tension. We also shared a life-long love of music: he sang and did voice work for local ads. But barely perceptible expectations or memories jostled over the table between us. I couldn't process anything. I struggled to reconcile the man in front of me, a stranger with a big shiny persona, with the infant I'd carried and borne and loved for a few days oh so long ago. Whose loss had nearly destroyed me. Whose existence remained a secret in my family, an ancient and sturdy secret, one crucial to my family's lofty idea of itself. My surrendered son! The two of us together again at last, eating chicken enchiladas with taped mariachi music blaring in the background. The waiter mistook us for a married couple.

On my drive back home, across the Ben Franklin Bridge and onto the North South Freeway, my mind was as turbulent as the Delaware River I'd just driven over. I was straddling the two parts of my life, the before and after of my unmarried pregnancy and my secret son's adoption. Maybe I was splitting in two. Beneath me, felt but not seen, were the fog-misted decades, nearly five of them, during which I'd lived a lie, refusing, on the advice of my parents, religious counselors and all the adoption experts, to acknowledge the existence of my firstborn child, to get over my experience and move on. I obeyed. I tried. I tried so hard. But as I drove home, I felt an inchoate rumbling inside myself, maybe longing, the beginning of a deep emotional upheaval.

The night after our Mexican lunch, we met for dinner at a Malaysian restaurant in Philadelphia's Chinatown. This time my son brought along his girlfriend, a chef, and I brought my raised son Gabriel, eighteen years younger, and his father, Dennis Chang, my stalwart friend, and still my husband, though by then we lived apart.

At the bustling industrial restaurant, my reconnection with Angus, who was no longer Angus, went more smoothly. Our other loved ones helped us to absorb some of our unsettled energy, to fill the canyon. I relaxed. My lost son was no longer lost!

We enjoyed a long and happy dinner, lubricated with BYO wine and beer. We dined on roti canai, satay and other Asian treats. We took happy smiling photos on a sidewalk outside and eventually said our reluctant goodbyes, promising to keep in touch. Deep in my bones I knew that I was about to emerge from the lies and secrets that had hurt me and constrained me my entire adult life. A dream was coming true. I'd be able to feel whole.

I do not in any way wish to intrude upon your life. I suspect I have found the right person. I would love to hear from you at least to confirm you are my birth mother.

When my son wrote these words he must have believed he'd be no more than a minor annoyance, like those door-to-door salesman who used to show up at your door peddling magazines or frozen gourmet dinners just when you're putting supper on the table.

I do not in any way wish to intrude upon your life.

No hint in his words that he understood that his reappearance in my life after so many decades might blow up my house and me with it.

I didn't either. I was shaken, but also thrilled. I'd never stopped longing to reconnect but had, many years earlier, given up hope of ever doing so. I'd finally understood that closed adoption as practiced in the United States was geared to complete severance and erasure.

Even so I had tried to search for him back in the 80s, soon after he turned 18. Commercial databases didn't yet exist and first mothers had no legal right (still don't) to any information about their relinquished children. Unless you had good connections working in adoption agencies, who could hunt for your records, or unless you were able to pay several thousand dollars to skilled adoption searchers who knew how to make their surreptitious way through a maze of legal obstacles, searching was almost always futile.

In 1985, I knew nothing about those secret searchers and I didn't have the money anyway. My only option to write to Catholic Charities in Boston, the agency I was certain had brokered our transaction. I wrote requesting whatever non-identifying information they could legally share about my son. I also said that I was willing to be contacted if my son ever made such a request. Catholic Charities replied that they had no record of his adoption.

CATHOLIC · FAMILY · SERVICES

55 LYNN SHORE DRIVE
LYNN · MASSACHUSETTS 01902
(617) 593-2312

6 SALEM STREET
READING · MASSACHUSETTS 01867
(617) 942-0690

February 4, 1985

Ms. Julia Chang
19 Constitution Blvd.
Berlin, N. J.   08009

Dear Ms. Chang:

I am writing to inform you that Catholic Family Services has
no record that your adoption took place through this agency.

I am sorry Catholic Family Services was not able to help you.

Very truly yours,

Katie Anno

Katie Anno, Adoption Supervisor

cam

This reply devastated me. No record of my son's adoption! The more
I read and reread it, the more humiliated I felt. But I was also afraid that I'd
get into legal trouble if I kept pushing. (So many first moms, like me, believe
that.) I was also terrified of what might happen if my parents learned that I
was searching; if they figured out that I hadn't really forgotten and 'moved
on.' By then I was a grown woman, married and the well educated and well
employed mother of another child. Yet I remained irrational on this matter,
afraid of my mother and my father, afraid of another abandonment if they
realized I'd never forgotten my son and still longed to know him.

After receiving that letter from Catholic Charities, back in 1985, I began to wonder if, maybe, what I believed had happened hadn't happened after all. Maybe I had not had a child I'd given up to adoption. Maybe I was delusional. Crazy, like my parents said. Maybe my firstborn child was a figment of my overactive imagination. Or maybe the adoption had been illegal. Sealed into my chamber of silence, it seemed that no possibility, no matter how insane, could be excluded with any certainty. I gave up searching in anger, frustration and humiliation. From then on, for the next three decades, as I raised my other children, two girls and a boy, none of them aware of his existence, I struggled with tidal anguish, forever ebbing and flowing. Then he found me.

For days after our reunion in Philadelphia, I was aloft. I was on the verge of a great healing, a reconciliation, not just with my surrendered son but also with my spouse, my other children, and with myself. (Oh, my other children! The deepest loves of my life and yet, following the dictates of those with so much power over me, I had deceived them!) But I now believed that I'd be able, at long last, to integrate the rebellious girl I'd been with my devoted, hard-working adult self. To explain myself to those I loved so much.

Life went on as I waited for my son's promised call. As I waited, a dream of happy family shined brightly in my imagination. Soon we'd all be together at the table, a complete family, sharing a scrumptious meal I'd prepared, lasagna, maybe or Ina Garten's roast chicken. I waited and waited for his call. Then I tried calling him. He did not answer – not on the first or second or seventh ring. I tried again and again, left messages, but he did not return my calls. Nor did he text or e-mail me. He didn't respond when I texted and emailed him. Eventually I got it: my son had ghosted me.

The Vow Of Silence

I always knew I'd given up a baby, a son. Despite the attempts of everyone around me to keep me quiet and erase my experience, I never forgot him, or the experience of his surrender. The last time I'd seen my baby was when I handed him over to the caseworker in a fluorescent-lit hospital corridor not far from an elevator. I was still bleeding, and my throbbing breasts were bound to stop lactation. I was exhausted from my long labor and my fight to see and hold my baby. I watched as if encased in ice as she went off with him bundled in her arms.

After Angus was taken away, my father and mother drove me back to our home in Plainville, Massachusetts, a mid-century rancher set into a hillside above the town's busy main street, a house much too small for our family of ten. It was the ninth home we'd lived in because Daddy, a public school administrator, was always changing jobs.

Silence all the way as my parents drove me back to Plainville. No words of comfort or solace, not one word. But after a lifetime of being rebuked by them, hidden in the infant asylum, and going through childbirth alone, I didn't expect compassion.

When I walked into the house, six of my seven siblings acted as if I'd just come in from running an errand, grabbing a loaf of bread, say, at the convenience store. No one asked where I'd been or why I'd been gone so long. All were silent, as they remain today. Except for my baby sister Amy, who was six. She'd begged Ma and Daddy to leave up the Christmas tree for my return from wherever they said I'd been. When I walked in, there it was, glowing in the living room. Amy came to hug me.

From then on I was forced into a vow of silence, one more profound than that of the Carthusian nuns and monks back in the Dark Ages. I took the vow under duress and in ignorance. I didn't understand how it would bind my life in shameful secrets, the secret itself never acknowledged. I took the vow without realizing that it would result in my lifelong struggle with insomnia, anxiety, depression and, at times, an enduring sense of betrayal with no understanding of its source, or its dimensions. I took it because I had no power to do otherwise. I took it in exchange for being allowed back home, back into my family, not welcomed, not really, not ever, only permitted to return to our house of a thousand sorrows.

Postpartum soon after turning 19, I struggled to go on with my life. Everything related to my son's existence slipped into a lacuna, one wrought by an unholy trinity of family, church and state. Silence and forgetting were its aims. No surprise that my parents wholeheartedly endorsed this. My son was never spoken of and my experience was never acknowledged, not by anyone, ever. I never saw his birth certificate or any other documents related to his birth or surrender. No photographs. No voluntary termination of my parental rights. Hence, no recorded evidence of my son or my experience, whatever there might have been, all sealed by the courts in Suffolk County, Massachusetts.

No documents, no records. No paper trail.

Even so, I had my anguish and my changed body, my shameful, sinful body, my devastated body. From then on I learned to keep it to myself. My son's birth and loss had happened in my body, and in my mind and my heart, and all were changed forever. I mourned my baby ever after even though I had neither documentary evidence of his existence nor any words to describe my loss. Despite my family's refusal to acknowledge him or my experience, and my caseworker's incessant declarations that I'd soon forget all about him, I didn't. I couldn't. I never did.

After my son went silent my heart was torn open. Soon I'd learn that such silences are more common than not in mother-child reunions. I'd learn that ghosting is a common theme in them. First mother and relinquished child come together and push apart as if in a repulsive field called diamagnetism, the opposite of magnetism. I'd learn that most reunions eventually fail, because either the searcher or the target (me, I'd been the target!), or both, are unable to negotiate the complex emotional territory of love, loss, loyalties, secrets and denials common to closed adoptions. They happen because one or the other (parent or child) is unprepared and cannot manage the upheaval of reconnecting. Most reunions, freighted with complexities, are scuttled by confusion, miscommunication and mistrust.

Reunion, after all, probes with razor-like tentacles the deepest parts of oneself and one's place in the world. It is an experience without parallel, most therapists agree. Leslie Pate Mackinnon, a birth mother and nationally recognized therapist specializing in adoption reunions, cautions about the potential dangers of reunion in adoption. "It's impossible," she said in an email interview, "to gauge the powerful impact of reunion without first comprehending the staggering degree of the original loss." That's what I, unbeknownst even to myself, was about to confront. The original loss.

As for the moment of actual reunion, that first experience of seeing one another, Mackinnon said her clients most often describe it as surreal. Surreal, as in having the quality of a dream, an experience you cannot believe is real.

When I opened my son's first email, I didn't know any of this. I never would've guessed that reconnecting with my lost child could shatter the foundations of my adult self. All I knew was that my lifelong dream of reconnecting had come true. Those fantasies of happy family had filled in my mind and heart. Then, in the wake of my son's inexplicable silence, they were blown to bits as if by an improvised explosive device. I was, all over again, bereft, as if I'd just handed him off to the caseworker. My ghost baby, gone again.

The psychologist Marilyn J. Mason, in her 1993 article, *Shame: Reservoir for Family Secrets*, argues that a dynamic crisis is often required for us to awaken to deeply buried pain. All my life I'd harbored pain. I knew that much about myself. How else to explain my debilitating bouts with anxiety and depression? But the source of my pain remained unclear, lost in the fog, and no therapist had been able to locate it.

The ghosting proved to be my dynamic crisis. Afterward, I began to glimpse, through the tunnel of time, my younger self. There she was, teenage Julia, waddling around the home for unwed mothers with her disgraceful belly. What a fall from grace she'd had, this vibrant creative girl! Surrounding her was an aura of shame as red as the letter on Hester Prynne's dress. She was still a teenager, but she was emotionally younger than her years, and she was angry, so angry. Why? I wondered when I saw her. I didn't understand her rage. I only saw that she was trapped in that asylum with no plan of escape and no grasp of what would happen next.

Decade after decade, as I completed my education, married, had other children, and moved into my grownup life as a wife, mother, writer and writing teacher, patching together my ever-precarious life with the big secret at its core, I'd ignored her. I could not bear to see her. Now she was right there, in my conscious mind, demanding recognition, the sad girl I'd left behind in the home for unwed mothers, the girl I used to be. That's when I realized that my hidden experience, (no light or air for almost half a century), was very much alive inside me. It was knotted close to my heart in a place where time never passes and nothing ever heals.

I had kept my shameful secret for most of a half century. I kept it because I was not able to dispute what the grown-ups told me back when I was weak and confused with only a gauzy sense of self: the revelation of my secret would destroy me. These words fossilized inside me, forming the bedrock of my adult life. The hidden girl had to be kept hidden.

But, in the wake of my son's silence and my lifelong reticence about my experience, my emotional struggles took on the glow of revelation. What had happened to me? More than half of my lifetime after the fact, this question formed itself and pummeled me. It threatened to break me. I knew I had to answer it, not just for myself, but also for my other children and my children's children.

I experienced an overwhelming need to reframe my life, to correct it, to come clean about the secret, one I had not chosen to keep but one that had been imposed on me when I was a depressed and forlorn teenager. Hovering around this secret, an ever-present nimbus, was the threat of familial abandonment, the loss of love, of familial connection, even long after my parents had died and my many siblings moved on into their own adult lives.

The poet C.K. Williams has used the term narrative dysfunction to describe how people lose track of their own stories, how their stories disappear into the rarely questioned narratives of mass culture and/or religious belief. To that I will add family orthodoxies. Somewhere among these three forces I'd lost my story.

In the wake of my son's silence I decided to take my story back, to seize it from the faith and culture in which the main events were set and to bring it back home to myself. I had to make things right. I knew it would be hard. (I didn't know how hard.) I also knew that I had to do it for the sake of my other children and my grandchildren. Narrative coherence in my own life: that's what I was after. A story that made sense.

Learning Curve

I did not search for another therapist. I realized by then, after working with half a dozen, that they could not help me find the answers. I've learned since that very few therapists have training in the kind of complex trauma experienced by mothers of adoption loss. They are not trained to recognize the unique forms of post-traumatic stress disorder we experience, let alone untangle what is now defined as disenfranchised grief, a quality we legions of birth mothers share. Disenfranchised grief is what happens when someone experiences a deep loss but is not allowed to mourn it, a loss that goes unacknowledged by the culture and those closest to her. It often encloses a big secret. It is life changing and lasts a lifetime.

So, no, I did not seek another therapist. Instead I read and researched as a way to steady myself and understand my experience. First I read adoptee Ann Fessler's essential and superb oral history, *The Girls Who Went Away* and then birth mother Karen Wilson-Buterbaugh's *Not by Choice*. I read and reread therapist and adoptive mother Nancy Verrier's perennial bestseller *The Primal Wound* about what happens to an infant when separated from its mother by adoption shortly after birth. I read the brilliant B.J. Lifton's groundbreaking nonfiction trilogy *Twice Born: Memoirs of an Adopted Daughter; Lost and Found, the Adoption Experience* and *The Journey of the Adopted Self*. These profound books helped me to retrieve puzzle pieces in my story. I also read scholarly articles, academic theses and a score of birth mother memoirs, a subgenre of its own if a quick Google search is to be believed. Most of these are self-published by untrained writers determined to reclaim the story of their lives. Every one of them is heartbreaking.

I studied the scholarly writing of historians Regina Kunzel and Rickie Solinger as well as treatises by the leading post-war adoption advocates, those who advocated for closed newborn adoption, among them Edna Gladney, who oversaw an eponymous chain of unwed mothers homes in the Southwest, and Rose Bernstein, a social worker at the Boston Crittenton home, both of whom became celebrities through their writing and public speaking about unmarried motherhood and newborn adoption.

In 2018, a turning point, I joined Concerned United Birthparents (CUB), a national advocacy group dedicated to supporting birth parents, and keeping families together. The group has existed since the mid-1970s, created by birth mothers in Boston, but I didn't know about them. Drawn by Ann Fessler (*The Girls Who Went Away*), that year's keynote speaker, I attended CUB's annual retreat in, of all places, Safety Harbor, Florida. That's where, for the first time, I "came out" as a mother of adoption loss. For the first time in my life, in an experience that inspired me and opened me to my own past, I listened to other birth mothers tell their stories. I didn't share mine, the hidden girl, still afraid, stayed mostly hidden, but for the first time in my grown up life I felt connected to others who'd had experiences like mine. I was not alone after all.

That 2018 CUB retreat in Florida opened me up to the territory of adoption loss and to my own past. The retreat presenters and the anecdotal experiences shared by many attendees left me with two ideas that quickly planted themselves deep inside my brain: first, that all adoption begins in loss, and second, that adoption is a permanent solution to a temporary problem, the biological parents' lack of resources. These evident truths, who can deny them, had never before occurred to me. They turned on its head the win-win adoption myth that I had accepted for most of my life, the one I'd been fed when I was a broke and broken pregnant teenager, a terrified girl with no supporters anywhere. Adoption begins in loss!

Adoption is a permanent solution to a temporary problem! After that first CUB retreat, as these ideas took hold inside me, it began to dawn on me that maybe, after all, I wasn't a just feckless slut who deserved severe and lifelong punishment.

By the time I returned from that first CUB retreat, my quest for an answer to the question, what had happened to me?, had escaped my pre-frontal cortex, a place of logic and coherence. It was seeping, instead, out of my amygdala, that primitive and often incoherent repository of anxieties and threat. As if with a dimmer switch touched upward, my buried past began lighting up.

I was entering the shadowy woods of birth mother loss, a place I'd never allowed myself to go. That's where I discovered my never acknowledged history of emotional and physical abuse in my first family. Where, before I could write about my pregnancy, I had to acknowledge how badly my parents had mistreated me, which I'd never before admitted, and scares me even now. I had to acknowledge, too, how the roiling turmoil in my family reflected many so aspects of the patriarchal world, a place of top-down authority. Gradually, and very painfully, I recalled the long-denied events leading up to the loss of my child. Some memories emerged in vivid color, as if they'd been waiting for me to find them. Some came back like journal entries, already written. But those most deeply buried and vulnerable to disregard, were blurred, indistinct, uncertain, the ones that cause my recurrent nightmares of shame and loss.

As I hunted, Daddy appeared to me, my loved and hated father. He warned me off my quest. "You have hurt your mother so badly," he said. "You almost killed her. You must not ever speak of this again." Daddy, the great secret keeper, whispered, the way he always uttered his most important words. "You've shamed and degraded us so badly that you must not ever speak of this again. If you want any kind of future, you must go on with your life as if this never happened. Nobody will ever love you if they know the truth."

I ignored my father's primal warning. I refused to give up my story the way I'd given up my son. I kept going back into the woods. Every time I did, another memory assailed me, and a familiar icy vapor wrapped around me, as if I'd stepped back into the dim foyer of St. Mary's Infant Asylum, the place of exile and secrets.

PART TWO

The Republic Of Shame

I n the fall of 1966, Daddy drove me to a century-old cloister in Dorchester, a sprawling northern neighborhood of Boston. Once the Georgian mansion of a wealthy family, the Diocese of Greater Boston had purchased it early in the 20th century, and repurposed it into St. Mary's Infant Asylum, a home for unwed mothers. It shared an urban campus with St. Margaret's Lying in Hospital, a prestigious maternity hospital, one of the few in the country dedicated to the care of mothers and babies. [1]

I was the salutatorian of the Class of 1965 at King Philip Regional High School in Wrentham, and Daddy was the superintendent. I should have been starting my sophomore year on scholarship at the University of Massachusetts in Amherst. Instead I'd be hidden at the infant asylum until I gave birth. The Daughters of Charity of St. Vincent DePaul would watch over me, monitoring my every move. I'd do penance for my many sins, and seek redemption, while awaiting the birth of my child who'd immediately be given up for adoption.

Daddy was imposing, bespectacled. He wore a good felt fedora pushed back on his head and drove hunched over the steering wheel of our new Chevy Bel Air station wagon. It was white, with oxblood vinyl upholstery, a nine-seater, just big enough to transport his spouse and brood. He'd have opted for the V-6 model, not the V-8, for its better mileage. *Who needs all that power?*

---

1 Among many notable patients, Rose Kennedy gave birth to Teddy at St. Margaret's. Marty Walsh, the former Boston mayor, Biden cabinet member, and current executive director of the National Hockey League's Player Association was born there, too. So were the infamous Wahlberg brothers Mark and Donnie.

Just the two of us on this journey to the far side of the city: Daddy and me, the second oldest of his eight, the one who'd caused him, he never tired of telling me, nothing but anguish and anger for my entire life so far. *Now this.* The air between us roiled with fury, closing in on despair. I couldn't look at him. I pretended I couldn't see him, couldn't hear him.

Why can't you just be good? Why can't you?

Granted, that spring I flunked out of U. Mass, a school I hadn't chosen and never wanted to attend, earning not a single academic credit second semester. *Who do you think you are, wasting my hard-earned money? You'll pay back every penny.* Daddy made this enraged vow when he saw my grade report, before he could have imagined that, just weeks before coming home, I'd gotten knocked up by a boy I didn't love, a boy who was joining the marines and heading off to war.

Ages before our trip to Dorchester, with my third or fourth missed period, I knew that I'd gotten myself into big trouble, the biggest trouble a girl in the 60s could get into. My life as I'd always lived it, a packed schedule of study and work at local businesses and enforced religious practice (deepened and softened by my dance classes; my amazing fantasy life and hope, *that thing with feathers)* was over. But I was too immature, too naïve, to understand that the mess I'd made foreclosed the possibility of getting what, beneath my furious defiant façade, I longed for most of all: love, the feeling of being accepted and cared for. The father of my baby didn't love me. He'd made that crystal clear the last time I'd seen him. Which was the last time I would ever see him. I was on my own.

That September day, as Daddy drove the 35-mile stretch north and east from our family home to that other one, he repeated that I was, of his eight children, the "bad apple." I had to be plucked from the basket. He reiterated my many failings, and the gift (though it was costing him *a bundle*) that he was giving me, this chance, if I behaved and did my penance, to redeem myself.

Redeem yourself!! The words, sharp stones, rattled in my skull.

Those Daughters of Charity, he warned, wouldn't put up with any of my shenanigans.

Daddy's words swarmed around me, threatening countless stings, even though I'd heard them all before, so many times. Silent, no doubt sullen, so full of fear and confusion that even my eyes hurt, I sat beside my father, staring through the windshield toward the gleaming city up ahead. My whole life he'd scared me with his dictates and demands, his sudden bursts of violence, but now I sensed us moving into an even darker place. I was terrified. We seemed to be airborne. Maybe the station wagon was hydroplaning though the sun shined hot and bright. I couldn't get my bearings. Couldn't stay put in my body. I escaped it, a trick I learned that summer: leave the body. Float nearby. Watch, but disconnect from everything. Above all, do not show any feelings. I became an expert at this last. I kept my feelings (fear, anger, sorrow, confusion, despair, others I couldn't name,) nested inside close to my gestating baby.

Why can't you just be good? Why can't you?

I did not have an answer. I thought I was good. I couldn't think of anything that made me bad except, maybe, for my super power, which was my ability to see through all the funky bullshit in the world and most especially through the many hypocrisies of my parents. Spouting love and peace in church and beating the crap out of us at home. Daddy liked to disparage me as a "smarty pants," a "know-it-all." Maybe that's what made me "bad."

In retrospect I note my mother's absence on this journey to the home for unwed mothers. At the time this was not remarkable. By the time I left, she'd shunned me. She'd wiped her hands of me, as if I were a pot she no longer had a use for, one she slammed against the counter in frustration a few times before tossing it into the trash. I no longer existed for her, a position she'd maintain throughout my ordeal and for years afterward. She never acknowledged that I'd borne a child I gave up to adoption or offered a word of understanding, although, as soon as I came home, she gave me an expensive girdle and told me to wear it all the time, "so nobody will know."

Ma's refusal didn't bother me: my life was over or would be soon. I was sure of it. Maybe, like my maternal grandmother, I'd die during childbirth. (I knew she had, though my mother never spoke of it, one of many silences and redactions in our family history. My mother was an orphan.) Death in childbirth, this struck me when I thought of it, as the perfect solution to my dilemma. What a relief! Goodbye to everything.

By the time I showed up with my swelling belly and my anguish, countless other unmarried pregnant girls had already passed through its doors and left without their babies.

Daddy gestures toward the station wagon door on my side. He doesn't plan to walk me in. I don't expect him to. I reach into the back for my suitcase and get out. I head toward the ornate front doors with my suitcase, my swelling belly and my anguish. It doesn't occur to me that countless other unmarried pregnant girls have already passed through its doors and left without their babies. Daddy calls out one last warning: "You'll have plenty of time here to think about the mess you've made. About who you are and where you want to go in your life. Don't waste it." Then he's gone.

St. Mary's Infant Asylum is dark as twilight and smells of myrrh and ash, lingering, maybe, from some recent ritual. As I walk inside, bright sunlight dims to cool shadows. My eyes water. I move into the shadows feeling like I'm plummeting through time, falling back into the Middle Ages, me, the dancer and poet, the wild child rebel who loved to laugh and longed to be on the cutting edge of everything. This might be the moment when "we" split apart: the me I started out to be and the one I would become. My super power fades. I feel it draining out of me, no recharge available.

Anxiety, an icy vapor, wraps around me as soon as I step inside, one I'd carry with me decades into my future. The black-clad Mother Superior, her face a quivering yolk within a stiff white wimple, leads me to my barren room, three cots in a row, a crucifix above each one. "Don't talk to the others about yourself," she says. "Never tell anyone your last name." Doing so, she points out, would sabotage the point of my confinement. Secrecy must be maintained at all times, or all would be lost. I'm not sure what 'all' consists of. I figure it must be my life, my future, that misty place up ahead, adulthood, in which I could not see a thing.

That early fall day, in my cell-like room at the infant asylum, I arranged the contents of my little suitcase: bras and panties I couldn't imagine ever fitting into, baggy pajamas and voluminous muumuu dresses I'd sewed from Simplicity patterns, hiding the illustrated pattern envelopes from my many siblings. My surroundings were intimidating, eerie, but not unfamiliar. I'd grown up in a house of spirits, after all: God the Father; Jesus, God's only begotten son, and Mary, the Blessed Virgin Mother (BVM), were omnipresent in our homes. A crucifix over every bed, (the crown of thorns, the nails in Christ's hands and feet, the sword hole in his side). The BVM here there and everywhere, images and statuettes in her favored iterations: Our Lady Queen of Heaven, Queen of Peace; Mother of Mercy, Mother of Sorrows; Blessed Mother; Our Lady of Perpetual Help. A golden halo always shined around Mary's bowed head and her fine blue robes shimmered. Sometimes a vanquished serpent (Satan), its fanged mouth wide open, writhed beneath her sandaled feet.

In the coming weeks and months, I would sleep in this room with two other girls but would have no recollection of their faces or their names, of how old they were, when they had their babies or if the babies were boys or girls. I wouldn't remember when or if they would leave to be replaced by another devastated girl. All of that remains a blank. Hence, I kept their secrets, whoever they might have been.

We had so much in common, we inmates or whatever it was they called us. All of us were middle-class white girls whose families had the means to take us out of the ordinary world and conceal us there, so that we could go back to our old lives. That's what we were told, and what many of us believed, we were in the process of redemption, a release from our past errors and sins, but we were silenced by our situations. We remained strangers to one another.

In that dim light, I sat on the hard mattress at the end of my unfamiliar bed and tried to pull myself together. Daddy's final warning echoed and repeated, *You'll have plenty of time here to think about the mess you've made. About who you are and where you want to go in your life.*

And I did. Or I tried to. Think about the mess I'd made. I tried to control my trembling fingers but could not stop my thrumming blood. Perhaps I thought about love, aware in a vague way that I lacked it, and that my craving for it brought me to places where I could not possibly find it. I wondered if I knew anything about love. I glimpsed but only briefly my baby's father, his face half hidden behind a veil of smoke. Loathing stabbed me. I tried to cut out the image and the loathing. Maybe that's when I realized I knew nothing about love. I didn't possess even a superficial understanding of what love required or what it offered in return.

Fear and anger swirled inside me. I couldn't sort out the mess I'd made and I could no longer imagine anything about who I wanted to become. My dreams of making my mark as a great artist, a dancer or a poet, had already vanished although I didn't quite realize that yet. But I understood more deeply than I wanted to the sin/penance binary into which I'd been shoved. I'd been steeped in it my whole life. Even so, this version was terrifying: the darkness, the ever-present sense of threat.

Sitting on the end of my designated cot, I didn't yet understand how completely my parents had ejected me from their care. I didn't yet understand that they'd handed me over to the machinations of church and state, and the era's established protocols for dealing with out of wedlock pregnant girls. I didn't yet understand that my fate had already been decided, and perhaps my parents didn't either. Maybe from the confines of their rigid faith, their striving middle-class lives, their never-verbalized commitment to patriarchy, they truly believed they were saving me. Killing me to save me.

Soon enough a little bell rang. It signaled my first supper in the basement cafeteria of St. Mary's.

The basement cafeteria of St. Mary's Infant Asylum is a dark humid place. Cinder block walls, linoleum floors, high narrow windows through which nothing can be seen. It stinks of pungent foods, meat loaf and tomato soup, Salisbury steak and boiled Brussel sprouts, and also of our anguish, a metallic taint in the thick air. The first sight of all of us together stuns me, a horde of 60 or 70, young and younger, from 13 to early 20s, with big and bigger bellies. How did this come to pass? All of us knocked-up girls, confined togethe. Nobody will ever take our pictures.

What I see is up close, deeply personal, but I'm detached from it at the same time. A shimmering red light of shame surrounds every one of us. Even at a glance I understand that every one of us is paying dearly for our stays and for our sins. We're preparing to give up our babies, as if such an action can ever be prepared for. But we have no idea what this will mean as we go on with our lives.

Just like in school we lined up with trays on the cafeteria line. We were handed our plates from a steam table. No choice; take what you get. Mystery meat. Soggy vegetables. A slice of white bread, no butter. We sat in silence at tables for eight, bowed our heads for grace (*Bless us, O Lord, and these thy gifts*) before the first bite. That first day I had no idea what I was putting into my mouth. But I realized, stomach quivering, threatening eruption, that I'd entered a circumscribed world, a foreign land, a place where no photographs would ever be taken. The Republic of Shame.

Surrounded by other girls and women I was alone, lost in this peculiar darkness, cut off from everything familiar and everyone I knew.

Abandoned. By my mother and father and my baby's father. But I didn't understand anything. My perceptions were as murky as the asylum's shadowy corridors.

So many of us wandered there but no one was keeping track. No laws required anyone to keep track. We'd been banished from our families, and almost all of us had been rejected by the fathers of our babies. We wandered in homemade maternity smocks or clothes left behind by other girls, usually in slippers, often on swollen feet, our arms around our own big bellies, comforting ourselves and the babies we carried, knowing we could not keep them but not knowing what that would mean.

On the wall of my office, I keep a small black and white snapshot of Ma and we three oldest girls, Jane, Veronica and me. In this photo, taken in the early '50s by my father, all four of us are squinting into the sun. We're trying to smile but look, instead, bewildered. Ma, implausibly young, poses with her hands upon the handle bar of a big baby stroller. Veronica, queenly, sits in it, her somber eyes as large and bright as sapphires. Jane poses on my mother's right, certain of her beauty. I, chubby and shy, am on Ma's left, my fists balled up in her skirt, my cheek against her thigh, as if trying to hide.

We girls are dressed alike in patent leather Mary Janes, white ankle socks, and ruffled dresses, sewn for us by my cherished paternal grandmother Nanny. No mistaking our resemblance: we are variations on a Celtic theme of plump cheeks, enormous eyes, strong chins, straight noses and abundant gleaming hair. My mother, though she does not show it, was well into her fifth pregnancy because my sister Leah is born a few months later.

I gaze at this photo, searching always for a meaning: a pretty young mother and her pretty well-dressed daughters. A photograph my father arranged and shot but from which he is absent. A snapshot in which we're trying to smile but look, instead, bewildered.

The Story Behind The Story

When I decided to write this story I wanted it to keep it simple. I envisioned a straightforward narrative about a witty and ambitious girl who got ahead of herself in the cultural confusions of the 1960s. A girl who longed to be on the cutting edge of every cultural change but who, instead, got "into trouble" and ended up pregnant in a home for unwed mothers. Who gave birth to a son under the most inauspicious circumstances and who signed away her parental rights when he was just three weeks old. That part of the story seemed as clear as water from a tap.

(The girl in that story was passive, acquiescent. She was mad with grief when they took away her son. Yet she accepted, as a matter of survival, her humiliation and degradation as a kind of penance, a necessary offering.)

But as soon as I began putting words onto the page, complexities piled up. I was, after all, revealing a secret that had festered in me for more than two thirds of my life, a secret that allowed me to remain a daughter in my family. Hidden within this revelation was my long buried rage at how I had been treated, both in my family and in the larger world; how I'd been trapped into the secret, one I'd never been able to reckon with.

Perhaps that's when I realized that the big secret about my bastard child also contained a host of smaller secrets, evasions and equivocations that twined like an epithelial tumor in my family's history and in the culture at large. Entangled too were religious beliefs, essential to any honest depiction of my experience. There was no "clear as water" story. Only a complicated many-layered story that switched back and forth in time.

From the start, I understood that my story was personal to me. It was unique in the way that every person's story is unique to his or her family, faith and time. But through my friendships with other birth mothers, and my attendance at our retreats and in support groups, my research and my growing knowledge, I began to realize that my story wasn't only mine. Rather, it reflected the stories of hundreds of thousands of other girls and women who lost their babies to secret adoption in the decades after World War II. Women who couldn't really explain what had happened to them and many who, at some point, gave up trying to.

My story also reflected, as if in a vast mirror, the century's feminist battles for reproductive rights and healthcare, ongoing battles over female fertility that have become political blood sport. I had so many questions about what had happened to me, but also to all the other unmarried mothers of adoption loss. Searching for the answers to these questions brought me face-to-face, ever so reluctantly, with forces that even now shape our views of female reproductive rights.

Days at the asylum are dark and chilly. Loveless days during which our every experience is intended to reinforce our unworthiness, our unfitness to become mothers. We're awakened in the early dark. We don't have alarm clock, don't need them. Rather, an ancient nun in a long black habit, a set of rosary beads hanging from her sash, walks up and down the gleaming marble hallways ringing a little brass bell. Her rosary beads clatter and the heels of her black brogues click against the floor. Like all the other nuns, this withered woman, a wraith, wears a gold band on her left ring finger to signify her marriage to Jesus. Her sole purpose in life seems to be to awaken us sleeping sinners. We always hear her bell because we cannot close our doors at night.

First thing every morning, six-ish, we walk to mass in a chapel on the grounds, our heads covered with white lace mantillas provided by the nuns. I see us in my mind's eye, flocks of us, all white girls, most of us under 20, processing in the early morning shadows to the chapel, in our baggy smocks and veils, then kneeling there on the hard wooden kneelers, hardly able to reach the prayer rail in front of us due to our massive bellies. We couldn't yet receive the sacrament, the Eucharist, because we'd be living in a state of mortal sin until we gave away our babies. Lord I am not worthy.

The constant ringing of Pavlovian brass bells keeps us on our daily schedules. They remind me, as they're intended to, of how, during mass, the bells are rung three times, each time to signify the calling down of the Holy Spirit. The presence of the Holy Spirit, via his daily visitations, is supposed to be a comfort to us in our time of need. That is what they tell us, but I am not comforted.

What We Carried

L ike all the other girls, I took my family background with me into the intimidating and stultifying rooms and corridors of St. Mary's Infant Asylum. Our family backgrounds shaped our experiences there, though we rarely shared them. We were too physically and emotionally blasted for that kind of sharing. Still it mattered.

I grew up in a rigid Catholic family, Scotch-Irish. My parents' faith, or maybe it was just their religious belief, was the shipping container (crowded, airless, no natural light) in which our family life played out. My mother married at 19. She was 21 when she had me, her second daughter. (Jane was 13 months older.) Ma had dropped out of nursing school to marry, and she "married up," to a well-educated man a decade older. She met him on a blind date arranged by his and her sisters, all of whom worked during the war at the Fore River Shipyard in Quincy, Massachusetts. My father's status, I understood as soon as I understood anything, was a matter of overarching importance in our lives. We four oldest girls were born in the first five years of my parents' marriage. Such extravagant fertility was common in the 40s and 50s when my parents, like their many brothers and sisters, made substantial contributions to the Baby Boom. My siblings and all three dozen of my first cousins were born between 1944 and 1963.

We were one of those good-looking-on-the-outside families, a signature of that era. My mother enjoyed her status as the wife of an important man and the mother of his children. Both parents reveled in their public image as the heads of a perfect American Catholic family, a pious and prosperous couple, the post-war ideal. Good looking and well turned out. No matter where we lived, everybody noticed us. So many people told me how lucky I was to be born into it. A different story played out behind closed doors. Or maybe the endless conflicts were the inevitable outcome of a family that demanded fealty to dogma with no allowances made for actual humanity.

Daddy, following an old Scots-Irish tradition, gathers us nightly for the family rosary: The family that prays together stays together. If you don't pray to his liking, if he suspects that you might not be sincere, if your voice isn't loud enough, he whacks you upside the head and you end up tasting carpet. The rosary: the Joyful mysteries, the Glorious mysteries, the Sorrowful mysteries. The Agony in the Garden, one of the Sorrowful mysteries, is the one my family is forever tangled up in.

Like most well raised Catholic girls of the Baby Boom, I grew up as ignorant of reproductive matters as it's possible to be. Ma had six more babies after me, but she never told me anything and I never asked. Neither did my father. I never witnessed physical affection between my parents. No hugs or kisses, nothing like that. Sexuality didn't exist in our family. Neither of my parents ever told me anything. After all, our only purpose in life was to know, love and serve God. No sex education required for that.

In the 50s and early 60s you could be ignorant of sexual matters in a way that's no longer possible. These days first graders know more than I knew in my teens. A federal law, the 1873 Comstock Act, outlawed both contraception and sex education. Hence reliable information was not available to us no matter how hormonal we boys and girls might have been. No social media. Mass media not yet an omnipresent force. My only sex education was gleaned from whispered conversations with friends who were as ignorant as I. (No sex education and no access to birth control. Yet the term "free love" glistened in the cultural conversation, alluring as a rare and precious gem, on the far side of the generation gap.)

Maybe my ignorance was intergenerational. At least six of us MacDonnell offspring were born with my mother under "twilight sleep." This combination of morphine and scopolamine was designed to reduce the pain of childbirth and alleviate the memory of it. It was very much in vogue in the 40s until the 60s, but it went out of favor because of its nega-tive side effects on mothers and their babies. Twilight sleep often triggered violent hallucinations during labor although the women had no memory of them afterward. This form of anesthesia during childbirth, like bottle-feed-ing afterward, kept women from experiencing too intensely the physical realities of parturition and its aftermath. I don't know if my mother chose to have it that way or if she just went along, unquestioningly, with the rec-ommendations of her male physicians.

Ma remained reticent forever about the physical realities of child-birth. She never told our birthing stories but it's possible that she did not remember them. Twilight sleep! Mystery and darkness around this most natural life-generating experience, childbirth!

Ma never explained the facts of life to me, not a word about men-struation or reproduction. Rather, through gossip with friends, I heard many peculiar and alarming rumors about what happened when you got your period. Until then, I imagined blood spraying from my vagina though I did not yet know the word vagina. (It was a mysterious place down there from which pee flowed several times a day. It was very close to the place from which shit fell.) Until I reached my teens I didn't know there was another opening. I didn't make the connection between menstruation and reproduction until my sister Jane gave me a church-published book-let about them. Until then, I didn't know that babies came into the world through the vagina, a fact my six-year-old grandson proudly announced to me not long ago when we were watching *Baby Boss* and the question, "where do babies come from?" came up. The "bah-china," he hollered with a happy smile.

Included in that stunning Catholic brochure was a mind-boggling explanation of intercourse accompanied by ridiculous black and white drawings of penises and vaginas. I was as repulsed as I was fascinated.

Ever so slowly I began to realize that my beloved movie and TV romances, along with the fictional love stories I read, inevitably ended up in the unfathomable to me physical reality of intercourse, a word never spoken in our household. At the time I couldn't imagine that my parents had ever engaged in such behavior. It was impossible for me to imagine that I ever would myself.

Ma never acknowledged that I got my period and I could not bring myself to tell her. Scared and ashamed, I threw away my first few pairs of blood-soiled underpants. I didn't know what else to do. I was 13. I told only my sister Jane, who gave me my first belt and sanitary napkins and told me how to use them and dispose of them. (We used the same brown paper bags in which we carried our lunches to school.) No tampons in our family!

Because there were so many of us, Ma marked our initials on our underpants with a black marker – for Jane and me our first two initials, Ja and Ju. Easier for sorting. "What's happened to all your underpants?" Ma asked me at some point. I couldn't say. I shrugged and she didn't press. "We're not made of money," she added. "I'm not buying you any more."

Red Lights and Erring Girls

I t came as no surprise to learn, during my research, that the seeds of what turned into the mass confinement of unmarried pregnant females and the closed adoptions of their newborns (the Baby Scoop!) were planted back in the late 1800s in the "red light" districts of major cities. This helped to answer the question of why, throughout my pregnancy and the termination of my parental rights, I was scorned as a whore. The seed planters turned out to be evangelical Christians, forebears of the folks agitating today to deny female reproductive rights.

Back in the 19th century, as recounted in Kunzel's essential history, *Fallen Women, Problem Girls: Unmarried Mothers and the Professionalization of Social Work, 1890-1945*, prosperous evangelical women participated, passionately, in that era's cult of "true womanhood." The most fervent among them took it upon themselves to "rescue" street-walkers from the alleys and tenements where they plied their trade. These missionaries intended to offer sex workers salvation, and to ensure their own, by transforming whores into good Christian women.

Prostitution wasn't yet a crime, but these self-proclaimed good (righteous) women launched a potent anti-prostitution drive, focused at least in part on controlling the spread of venereal disease among their husbands, sons and brothers.

Beginning the late 1800s, wealthy evangelical women disguised themselves in shabby clothing and walked the night streets of brothel districts. With printed brochures and verbal exhortations, they circulated among their "less fortunate sisters," encouraging them to come in from the cold, literally. To trade their "sinful" ways for the Christian ideal of female piety and goodness. They offered sex workers salvation, and intended to ensure their own, by transforming whores into good Christian women.

So potent was this anti-prostitution drive that wealthy male philanthropists funded the building of "rescue" homes across the country where "fallen" women could be sheltered, clothed and fed while they submitted, with the help of their female saviors, to repudiating their own corruption.

Throughout this decades-long effort, Kunzel notes, the rhetoric of "sisterhood" abounded among the fallen women and their rescuers but it obscured "the hierarchical nature" of the relationship between them. The rescuers, no surprise, saw themselves as far superior to those they were rescuing. And, as time went on, it became alarmingly clear that many "fallen" women did not wish to be rescued or transformed. They did not want to be rehabilitated into "good women," thank you very much. Though many of them tried the rescue homes, they stayed only for a short while, perhaps healing from an illness or regrouping financially, before they headed back out to the night streets. To the chagrin of their rescuers, this demonstrated that their "transformative redemptions" were only temporary.

The pharmaceutical millionaire, and evangelical zealot, Charles Nelson Crittenton was among the major early builders of rescue homes. (His philanthropy, the National Florence Crittenton Mission, now called the Florence Crittenton Agency, was named for a daughter of his who'd died in childhood. It still thrives in Knoxville, TN.) Another was the Salvation Army, founded in Great Britain by Methodist preacher William Booth, but finding its greatest success in the United States with its rapidly expanding chain of Booth rescue homes. (Alone among their contemporaries, the Salvation Army expressed a dual purpose in its rescue operations: that the care of the body "necessarily precedes the salvation of the soul.")

But by the early 20th century, the well-heeled evangelists had become flummoxed by the defiance of sex workers who did not wish to be saved. On their nightly walks, the rescuers couldn't convince enough working girls to come into a shelter or to stay long enough to experience "true redemption." As quoted by Kunzel, one Crittenton worker declared that the effort and money invested in transforming prostitutes into good women was all out of proportion to the results achieved.

Eventually the frustrated do-gooders faced what Kunzel calls "the bottom line" imperative of empty beds. That's when they turned their missionary gaze to unmarried pregnant girls, some of whom were prostitutes, but others, in a growing phenomenon, were girls from "good" families. Disobedient daughters! Naughty girls! So many of them!!

Such "erring girls," Kunzel writes, were soon discovered to be more pliable than the hardened professionals of the streets. They were found to be "more amenable to longer stays…(and) more receptive to the evangelical message."

Closed newborn adoption soon turned into big business for religion-based non-profits. Some three hundred maternity "homes" in 44 states thrived on both coasts and across the vast middle of the country. They ran at full capacity. Many had waiting lists! But court-enforced silence surrounded their stratagems.

Not until this era was over did a name for it emerge: The Baby Scoop. Despite its billowing numbers before and after World War II and right up through the war in Vietnam, it went mostly unnoticed. Potential traumas to first mothers and their disappeared children were never considered. Parents (like mine) determined to protect their familial reputations eagerly reinforced the lies, secrets and silence required of them. The first research into this phenomenon of closed newborn adoption didn't happen until the 1990s.

Before long, back in the day, other religious organizations, including Catholic Charities and Jewish Family Services, realized the benefits of sheltering unmarried pregnant girls. All shared a faith-based zeal to reform females who'd crossed the cultural line between good and bad. All benefitted financially (despite their non-profit status) from the many fees they could charge for their services. But the so-called "homes" never shook off the lurid glow of the red light district. I felt it my entire time in hiding.

In her scholarly paper *Pulp Fictions and Problem Girls,* Kunzel charts how popular magazines such as True Confessions and True Stories, with circulations of over one million readers, expressed the "increasingly hysterical concern of postwar Americans with female sexual transgression." Their stories about the perils of single pregnancy, such as *The Terrifying Ordeal of the Unwed Mother* (1949), offered what she calls the genre's "characteristic and profitable mix of titillation and moralizing."

The popular imagination, goaded by mass media, hadn't yet seized upon serial killers, pedophile priests and coaches, or mass shooters as the most evil among us. So it was left to unwed mothers (and JDs) to carry the culture's burdens of sin. Like the goat in Leviticus, we were sent out into the wilderness, the iniquities of mid-century transgressions heaped upon our backs.

When Daddy brought me to St. Mary's, I knew it was going to be a punishing place, like a jail. I understood that unwed mothers occupied the shadowy bottomland of the culture, close to juvenile delinquents (JDs!) and kidnappers. By the 50s and 60s, everyone understood this – even though the women themselves were silenced and, whenever possible, hidden.

As Kunzel recounts, trashy tabloids, newspapers, glossy magazines and low-budget "B" movies often focused on the transgressions of the wanton women who got pregnant, while various religious organizations, adoption agencies, and the administrators of the so-called homes proselytized about their own goodness and efficacy. They were good at denigrating and silencing the women whose babies they seized. They created, with stunning success, through the enduring pain of first mothers, the fairy tale of adoption as a win-win for everyone involved. They did this by eliminating first mothers from the story. They disappeared us, hiding us away in that lightless place, the republic of shame.

Even as the culture was wracked by upheavals toward the end of the 20th century, girls who "got into trouble," still became outcasts; fallen women in need of redemption, as they'd been for centuries. The men and boys remained free to fuck around as much as they wanted to without fear of censure (except, occasionally, by their own wife or a girl's father.) Mass sequestration of unmarried pregnant females, and the secret adoption of their newborns, morphed into a crude solution to what was believed to be the growing problem of slutty girls. In post-war America, Kunzel, writes, "single pregnancy was so markedly stigmatized …that most women did what they could to cover their tracks."

By the time, in the late 60s, I stumbled onto the scene, hapless, brainy and unloved, even by myself, newborn adoption was a lucrative and highly praised enterprise but also unknown to me. With birth mothers shamed and shoved into the shadows, and their children unable to speak for themselves, the divine myth of closed adoption as a win-win had become accepted as true. In the pre- and post-World War II years, the myth became so potent it dazzled everyone, many birth mothers included. By the time that epoch ended in the early 70s, with the sudden widespread availability of The Pill, and the passage of Roe V. Wade, it's estimated that between 1.5 and 4 million new mothers had given up newborns to nonfamily closed adoption. My son was one of them.

No federal laws ever mandated record keeping for adoption, and state records were notoriously careless or corrupt. Hence, the arc of the adoption story was controlled completely by those who brokered them: religious organizations, adoption agencies and state-run child welfare agencies, along with the parents of the mothers, and sometimes the young mothers themselves, who'd been "rescued" and "redeemed" via the surrender of their babies. These made up what I call the unholy trinity of closed adoption, an impromptu and synergistic gathering of powerful forces even though they were never officially connected.

Transubstantiation

I knew from the moment I got to the asylum that my son's birth certificate would be changed when his new family took possession of him. Took possession!! To my 18-year-old mind, changing the birth certificate didn't seem like a big deal. I was blind to its ramifications. I could not and did not imagine a child's desire to connect with his or her genetic roots. I could not imagine how these changed birth certificates would wreak havoc in the lives of adoptees.

Nobody explained the reasons for amending the birth certificates to me and it did not occur to me to ask. We girls did seem to realize, without ever talking about it, that the birth certificates had to be changed so that all traces of our quasi-criminal motherhood would be removed. We accepted the idea that the change was necessary in order for our children to have fulfilled lives unstained by our transgressions.

Only decades later, when I entered the dark woods of birth mother loss, searching for an answer to the question of what had happened to me, did I begin to question this longstanding practice.

The answer tracked back more than 80 years. That's when the unholy trinity came up with a brilliant sleight of hand, one that enabled an explosion of closed infant adoptions, concealing and/or stealing the genetic identities of countless babies. That's when powerful people working on adoptions, insisting that adoptive families were exactly like biological families, decided to replace the original birth certificates of bastard babies with "amended" versions that identified only the adoptive parents. The changed birth certificates were never labeled "amended." Rather, the parents were listed as if they'd conceived the child in question. Moreover, adopting parents had no legal obligation to reveal the truth to their children and many of them never did. The same powerful people (think Unholy Trinity) then convinced the family courts in counties of jurisdiction to seal the original birth certificate (OBC). The changed birth certificate was intended to hide, forever, the biological identity, and thus the illegitimacy, of the adopted child.

Adoption agencies, adoptive parents and religious organizations continue to passionately embrace amended birth certificates citing the best interests of the child. This long accepted legal deception violates the United Nations High Commission on Human Rights and the U.N. Convention on the Right of the Child. It declares: 'The child shall be registered immediately after birth and shall have the right from birth to a name...' National governments, it states, must 'undertake to respect the right of the child to preserve his or her identity, including nationality, name and family relations..."

The United States is one of only two nations in the world that have not ratified the U.N. Convention on the Rights of the Child. The other is Somalia.

The practice of changing original birth certificates went mostly unchallenged until the '90s when adoption reform advocates, like Bastard Nation and the Adoptees Liberty Movement Association (ALMA), began demanding access to adoption records. These challenges have only intensified with the emergence, in the late aughts, of commercial DNA databases. These basic DNA searches, at a cost of about $100 to $500, have wreaked havoc on the traditional secrets and silence of closed adoption. They allow biological relatives to find each other no matter what obstacles church and state have placed in their way. They have resulted in countless surprise revelations. Immeasurable joy and sometimes shock and sorrow have ensued. Distant relatives, third and fourth cousins, follow genetic trails until, at long last, they find their parent or their child. Two never-before-heard-of categories have emerged: Late Discovery Adoptees, or LDAs. These are adoptees who remained unaware of their status until DNA results showed that the parents who raised them were not their biological parents. A devastating reality for as-yet-uncounted numbers of them. (More about another category, Not Parent Expected, very soon.)

None of that was ever dreamed of in the early decades of the 20th century.

Many social workers in the 1930s were involved in this drastic change in adoption law but social worker Edna Gladney was among the most effective and articulate advocates for this form of legal identity theft. She is said to have personally brokered 10,000 newborn adoptions. No whiff of scandal has ever attached itself to Gladney personally or to her still successful eponymous agency, the Gladney Center for Adoption in Fort Worth, among the most prestigious in the country. Quite the contrary, Gladney was esteemed as noble and selfless. A major 1941 film *Blossoms in the Dust* depicts her as the altruistic savior of countless orphans. Its star Greer Garson earned an Academy Award nomination for her performance as Gladney. It is still available for streaming on major platforms including Amazon Prime and YouTube.

Famously Gladney once declared, "There are no illegitimate children, only illegitimate parents."

Her words expressed the social attitudes of the time. They weren't merely embraced by the unholy trinity. They flared into fact for counselors and caseworkers across the country. Even now they glower in italic font on the website of the Gladney Center.

Gladney's philosophy was still in full flower more than thirty years later when my father left me off at the doors to St. Mary's. *No illegitimate children, only illegitimate parents.* I did not know it at the time but it's what overwhelmed me during my pregnancy, my time at the home, and the loss of my child. I was illegitimate. I have never fully recovered.

Once courts sealed those original birth certificates, biological mothers were written out of the adoption story. They did not legally exist. And, after being hidden and humiliated and coaxed or coerced into signing away their parental rights, shame shrink-wrapped them (us) into silence and burdened them (us) with lifelong anguish. Hundreds of thousands of birth mothers would never see or hold their babies or even learn their gender, a devastating mystery for she who holds it. About 40 percent would never have another child, a baffling form of secondary infertility. It is believed to be triggered by traumatic grief.

According to the most recent research, birth mothers' feelings of shame, guilt, anger and sadness, linger forever. They often reveal themselves in depression, addiction, troubled marriages and the overprotectiveness of their subsequent children.

I feel disgust and disapproval, a hobbling weight, the moment the big doors close behind me at St. Mary's. I feel the weight, one I will never fully shake off, but I can't decipher it. I can't wrap my mind around the reality that I, Julia (known to most as Julie or Jules), a smart artsy girl who loved to laugh and dance, the vibrant and aspiring second daughter in a much admired middle-class Catholic family, has suddenly been transfigured into such an execrable creature, no friends or allies anywhere. Incarcerated.

I didn't have a clue about any larger cultural meanings when Daddy left me off at the door to St. Mary's Infant Asylum. I was too young and naïve, too hurt, to see beyond my own situation. I would have been dumbfounded to learn that more than 85,000 other American girls, according to the University of Oregon's Adoption Research Project, relinquished their babies that same year, 1967, when I felt so alone and so ashamed.

But even if I had known, I wouldn't have been thinking about it. I was much too scared to think. I was twisting on the blade of what was going to happen to me next and how I would survive. Then, too, suddenly, I was afraid for my baby. At the time, I didn't recognize these potent feelings as the doubling that all mothers feel: love and worry. I've carried them with me ever since.

My last two years in high school I work at a pharmacy and soda fountain a short walk down the hill from where we live. The job gets me out of the house and pays for my dance classes. I enjoy serving customers coffee and pie in the afternoon; making them milk shakes and vanilla Cokes and lime rickeys. I enjoy chatting with customers, and organizing merchandise, especially the beauty products. I see married men come into the store surreptitiously and head to the back to see one of the pharmacists. I know they're buying condoms even though I never ring them up. I have some idea what condoms are or at least I think I do. The magazine racks become my portal to the amazing world I plan to enter. Life. Look. Vogue. Holiday. Saturday Evening Post. Photoplay. Mademoiselle. *I read them when business slows. Sometimes I buy them and bring them home in a plain brown bag. When I am alone, I absorb them on my bed in my room, enchanted by this world of art and beauty and glamour and higher consciousness. I know it exists if only I can find it for myself.*

Daddy goes to daily mass and hauls us off to Confession every week. Confession is preceded by the mandatory Examination of the Conscience, the tally of our sins. Daddy makes sure we remember all the bad things we did that week, the back talk and disobedience and disrespect of our parents; the squabbles with our brothers and sisters, our indecent thoughts. Daddy reminds us to be diligent in our Examination of the Conscience so we don't leave anything out. Then we head to church to tell our sins to the priest behind the dark screen.

Stories, Lost In Transit

I grew up in a family without stories. Or maybe fealty to Catholic dogma replaced the possibility of any other narrative. My relatives, so many of them, didn't talk about the past. They expressed no interest in their own stories, no apparent pride in their achievements. The bits I've gathered reveal a history of constant flight. My progenitors, their names uncertain, their faces unfamiliar, left Ireland and Scotland during the second half of the 19th century. They left in desperation, fleeing famine and disease, religious discrimination, abject poverty, hopelessness. Like countless others in that great diaspora, my ancestors likely dreamed archetypal dreams of a better life in a new world, a place of material plenitude, spiritual abundance, opportunity. But they left no record of it. They traveled far in their quest for these things, but they also traveled light. They left behind, time and again, all that might encumber them: books, furniture, utensils, clothing; relationships and memories of relationships, a sense of place, and their stories. They were forward-gazing people who didn't talk much about themselves and didn't talk about not talking. They kept moving forward, never looking back.

Daddy's family, as far as anyone surviving knows, alighted first in Nova Scotia, then roved down through New England and across the continent to the Pacific Northwest before finally heading back again to the South Shore of Boston, near the Fore River Shipyard, and the famous shoe factories (Bostonian in Brockton) where many found work. I know even less about my mother's family, the Cushings and O'Degans, except that, by the time of the First World War, they too were ensconced on the South Shore of Boston, and also earning livelihoods at the shipyard. It's where my parents met, on a blind date.

In the homes where I grew up, about a dozen of them, there were no chests, no chairs, no candlesticks, no brooms, bowls or Bibles passed down to us from previous generations. Neither of my parents possessed heirlooms from their families or mementos from their childhoods. We had no paintings or photographs of our ancestors, no images of those who'd gone before us, those whose genes and DNA we shared. Nor was there any talk of them.

Each time we moved, never with much warning, Daddy and Ma examined our belongings with sharp well-practiced eyes. And each time, it seems to me, we were stripped of our material attachments. Dolls, books, stuffed animals; diaries were trashed or left behind for the new family. Our grief over these losses could never be expressed, let alone acknowledged. *Stop that crying or I'll give you something to cry about!* My siblings and I, following a great family tradition, grew up detached from the past, from our feelings, and ignorant of our own history. Silent.

Before I took up residence in the Republic of Shame I fought hard to be myself, to become myself, a lively and creative girl, even as I felt, in some vague and unacknowledged way, that I might be in danger. Our family's life was one of constant uprooting, dictated by Daddy's wanderlust and his incessant climb up his career ladder. I was always struggling to find a toe-hold for myself in my family and in the world. I had trouble finding space for myself. I thought I had found one when we were living in Bay Shore, NY, on the bay side of Long Island. I was in sixth grade, an adolescent, when we moved from upstate New York into a small 60s split-level in one of those vast developments built over the potato fields on Long Island. I'm not sure if Levitt built our development but, if not, it was a replica: miles-long grids of straight streets lined with identical split-level homes. Our stay there was merely an interregnum, a tumultuous one during which the conflicts between Jane and me escalated to dangerous levels, the two of us crammed into a cinderblock basement room next to the garage. Jane, beguiling and treacherous. I'd been twinned with her since I was born even though I now theorize that she, just a year old, must've been furious when I suddenly appeared taking up her spot in my mother's arms. I learned early that I couldn't trust a word she said. She pinched, scratched, hit, shoved, slapped and tickled. She bit and pulled my hair. She snooped and tattle-tailed. She got me into trouble more times than I can count, lying to our parents early and often, always managing to get herself off the hook. And there we were, at 12 and 13, stuck together, in that below-grade moldy room.

My reprieve came two years later when Daddy bought, in an estate sale, a big old Victorian house just steps from Great South Bay. Six bedrooms, three bathrooms, and a big two-story carriage house in the backyard, one that faced a service road and had actually been used for carriages, and domestic deliveries. It was the eighth home we'd lived in, the first house in which I had a room of my own. It was on the third floor, in the old maid's quarters: sloping ceilings, stained glass in the gable windows, and a big bathroom across the hall. Despite its cracked plaster, uneven floorboards, and sporadic heat, I begged my parents to let me have it. After Jane and mine's umpteenth shrieking fight, a bloody one that included a shattered bathroom window, and left a scar on my wrist, they agreed.

On Ocean Avenue, the backyards of the mansions across the street backed onto a canal, and docks at which owners could tie up their yachts and cabin cruisers. It was a short walk from our house to the public beach on Long Island Sound, which we did, every sunny day every summer.

We lived in Bay Shore for five years, from sixth grade until my sophomore year in high school. That's when, at a distance from my sister, I began to piece together an idea of myself as a smart artsy girl. She was loving and creative, this girl, a dreamer with many abilities, ambitious, bright and funny, a bit of a clown, curious and ever optimistic. She had lots of friends.

But the qualities she valued most about herself, her wit, her creativity, her thoughtfulness, remained the target of ridicule by her mother and her sister. They called her lazy and smarty-pants because she hated housework and loved to read. She avoided chores whenever possible by hiding with a book. Once, in a rage, her mother chased her through the house with scissors and cut off her long hair. Her father had nothing to say about that. Rather, he complained, early and often, that she lived in a dream world, her head forever in the clouds. She told him she liked the view better there.

By the time we got to Bay Shore, I lived to dance. The music and movement became the outlet for my yearning, and what I didn't yet know was my creativity. I'd started when I was a chubby toddler, maybe three or four years old. My sister Jane and I began dancing lessons together because my parents worried about my weight. (Chubby. I was called chubby which, to my young ears, was a fate worse than death.) My most vivid memories are of our recitals. We always had gorgeous costumes (bright blue satin sailor outfits with perfect little Dixie Cup hats or swirly pink princess dresses with tiaras) sewed for us by my beloved paternal grandmother, Nanny. But Jane would forget the steps, and giggle at the edge of the stage to great applause, while I went on twirling, leaping, tapping and shuffling off to Buffalo.

I kept on dancing after we left Weymouth, though Jane never danced again. Tap, ballet, acrobatics and jazz, I loved them all. Every time we moved I found a new dance teacher, an activity my parents agreed to as a weight control measure. (Each of my siblings got to have a music lesson' of one type or another. Clarinet, alto sax, drums and violin were among the instruments they played. My brother Gregory was a superlative trumpeter but gave up music before his professional career could blossom.)

In Bay Shore, my wonderful dance teacher Kay was an acolyte of Bob Fosse, who was just emerging as a force in dance. Kay was slender and silver-haired, she wore it short and spiky. Full of creative energy, she took me under her wing. Kay was the first of several teachers I had, in both academics and extracurricular activities, who cared for me and helped me to grow and develop in their field of expertise. Surrogate parents. I bent toward them like a plant to the sun.

I wanted to be just like Kay, in her purple leotard, a short black dancer's skirt, her black fishnet tights and black jazz shoes. I could walk to her studio downtown, a bright, mirrored space overlooking a shoe store, pharmacy and pizza joint on the busy main street. My parents didn't actually approve of Kay or of our sinuous jazzy dance moves, hips jerking and jutting, shoulders shrugging, head swiveling, but apparently my need for fitness overruled their misgivings. My favorite routine was to the theme song from Peter Gunn, with its distinctive guitar riffs. It was later appropriated, and hilariously revitalized, by the Blue Brothers.

Soon I became part of Kay's small company, performing in nursing homes, hospitals, fire stations and at various civic events. If I couldn't walk to rehearsals or performances, Kay drove me. Except for frequent battles over the cost of my leotards and many pairs of dance shoes (always second hand and even then a waste of hard-earned money) Daddy and Ma paid no attention to my dancing.

∞

In junior high and high school I developed a small group of friends who, like me, loved musical theatre and movies and pop music and trashy novels. We were marginal in school and cherished our marginalization. We did school shows together. We could sing every word of every song in *West Side Story* and recreated to great hilarity the choreography of Jerome Robbins. I always took the part of Bernardo, the leader of the Sharks.

Bay Shore High was a big competitive school where I earned honors in whatever the highest track classes were called back then. Daddy, an educator, never acknowledged my good grades. I never seemed to achieve anything worth his mentioning. At the time, I didn't care. I was far more interested in my social life than in academics.

My friends and I called ourselves the God Damned Independents, the GDIs, to thumb our noses at the popular girls in the sororities who'd never invite us to join them. We were too young to date, and weren't pretty enough, but we made our own parties, lively and loud. We had more fun than any other young teens had ever had, or so we thought.

As often as I was allowed, I slept over at my friends' houses though they never slept at mine. We'd binge on M&Ms and potato chips until we puked and watch TV until the stations signed off in the early hours of the morning. I glimpsed families different from my own. Among them were prosperous Jewish families in which the kids were lavished with affection. I tasted, for the first time, lox and bagels and cream cheese, and experienced family breakfasts where mother, father and children, enjoyed each other's company. They liked being with each other! I still have the gold locket the girls chipped in to give me when I moved, their names engraved on the back: Wendy, Janet, Sharon, Missy.

We moved away from Bay Shore the day after Christmas in the middle of my sophomore year in high school (1963). Just like that, boom, with little warning and no understanding, we left the house I loved in a place where I was happy and moved to a small factory town in southwestern Massachusetts.

The movers come before dawn. They empty out the house and haul away its contents. They are heading to our next house, 225 miles away. Daddy has accepted a position as the superintendent of the King Philip Regional School District in Wrentham, Massachusetts. I watch but can't quite believe this is happening, being snatched away from my loved world, my room, my dance teacher, my friends, my school. As I watch the movers move, a bad feeling floods me. I can't name it but I will carry it, like a crate from that abandoned home, for many years.

Upside Down House

After we settled in Plainville, my family, as if pulled by a rip current, slid deeper in the darkness and confusion of the world and our own conflicts. I couldn't see the current but felt its tug through my last years of high school. The world as I'd known it was quaking around us.

In that move from Bay Shore to Plainville, I lost my friends, my school, my dance teacher Kay. I lost Great South Bay where I could walk anytime I wanted to. The shimmering blue water, quiet under the dome of sky, the blurred horizon. But the biggest thing I lost was my own bedroom, the safe haven for my shaky sense of self. With the loss of my own room, I was lost. At least it felt that way when I was 15.

Our house on Pleasant Street still shimmers in my memory with its post-war modesty: blue-gray asbestos shingles with white shutters, a big picture window overlooking the sloping front lawn, the old oaks and maples arching above its black roof shingles, the turmoil inside. The pious, ambitious and domineering father, standing strong in the current, determined to fight the rip tide of change. The angry and overwhelmed mother, five children in the first six years of her marriage, and then three more, so many children she didn't know what to do. But she didn't even know what she was angry about. Later, much later in my life, I came to believe that Ma's self-knowledge was stunted by her submission to her assigned roles. She did not understand herself. How could she understand me?

It was, literally, a topsy-turvy house. Before we moved in, Daddy contracted with the local vocational high school to have the walkout basement transformed into four bedrooms, a bathroom and a laundry room.

These were the cheapest possible renovations: flimsy sheetrock, dropped ceilings, concrete floors covered with linoleum. No comfort or beauty anywhere. In that too-small house, we kids were doubled up in tiny spaces. I was forced back into sharing a room with my sister, a room so small we had to sleep together in a double bed. (We were 15 and 16.) She got the window side. She also got the only closet and bureau. My things were stored in the hall outside where they were rifled almost daily by mysterious trespassers.

I missed everything about my old life in Bay Shore and I longed to go back to it. I hated sharing that room with my sister. Even the memories cause bile to bubble up into my throat. I was full of rage and sorrow but I couldn't name those feelings. I just felt bad, all the time. But I wasn't allowed to express feelings about the move or the shared room. None of us were. Only my parents were allowed to have feelings but the only feelings they seemed to have were anger and frustration. I tried really hard to keep my distance. I got out of the house whenever possible.

In the upside-down house, Daddy was more determined than ever to control everything going on inside it. Nightly rosary. Weekly Confession. Mass on Saturday and Sunday. Maybe it was the craziness in the world (assassinations, race riots, serial killers, black men winning Oscars and Noble Peace Prizes) but my parents got crazier in Plainville. Ours became a Belfast of family life though I could not have made the metaphor back then when I was living it. It was a place of hidden allegiances, simmering conflicts, jealousies, secrets, betrayals and violence. This violence included both planned punishments, getting "the belt" from my father as a consequence for some infraction, perhaps "backtalk" to our mother or a missed curfew, and unpredictable outbursts, the quick smack upside the head triggered by a sudden unbearable frustration. Spilled milk at the family table was a frequent source of paternal rage. If one of us accidentally tipped over a glass at our crowded little table, we were smacked or humiliated. Both parents were also skilled name-callers: Fatso. Jackass. These names hurt more than anything. Not even for a nanosecond did I ever believe that children's rhyme: "sticks and stones will break my bones but names will never hurt me."

My siblings and I, as I saw it, were forever jockeying for favor from our mother and father who loved comparing us to one another. And we couldn't stop; we never have stopped, competing with one another for attention, privileges, and love.

Right away I plunged into life at King Philip, a school housing grades 7 to 12, where Daddy was the boss, and three of my sisters were also students. I ignored my sisters as much as possible even though we passed each other in the hallways, ran into each other in the cafeteria, and at our lockers and on the bus. Daddy made us take the bus like everybody else, a 45-minute ride, instead of driving to school with him, so that we wouldn't appear to be "privileged characters."

During those years in Plainville, I was trying to become me. I struggled to figure out who I was while the world I lived in, that small town, kept seeing me as just one of many MacDonnell girls, peas in a pod, a phrase I detested. We oldest four even looked alike, but I didn't want to look or be like my sisters. I didn't want to be mistaken for them and it upset me that I so often was. I did not want to be known as the super's daughter. More than anything I wanted to be recognized for who I was even if I was still mostly a blur even to myself. More than anything, I longed to be loved.

As soon as I could, I tried out for cheerleading and made the varsity squad. I loved it. This was the first of my attempts to "fit in" in my new school. But the next thing I knew, after our first basketball game, I was ejected from that little community of special girls, with our pompoms and pretty outfits. My father, behind my back, had told the coach, not me, that I was forbidden from participating. Daddy never explained and I didn't dare to ask.

My life went from bad to worse. Soon after that, practicing a backflip on the balance beam with the gymnastics team, I fell to the floor and fractured my skull. I was whisked off to the local hospital where I spent three weeks. After that, the doctors cleared me, but Daddy barred me from gymnastics. Then I tried out for a swim team in the town next door but didn't make it. Finally, during the summer between my junior and senior years of high school, I got a summer job as a lifeguard at Lake Pearl, a popular teen hangout. I was on top of the world. But my boss who happened to be a phys ed teacher at our school, fired me a week later. Daddy had, again behind my back, intervened. Later, in school, the teacher apologized to me.

That summer, instead of working at Lake Pearl, Daddy got me a job on the line at an eyeglass factory. The factory job, the first of several I'd experience, would give me a good dose of reality, Daddy declared. I spent the day putting tiny metal screws into the hinges of eyeglass frames. All I learned about reality is that it was a place I didn't want to be.

My high school days, after our move to Massachusetts, were days of struggle in the world, in my family, and inside myself. I got through them because of the solace I found in dancing and my dreamy dreams of somehow escaping to a better world than the one I was living in.

The Vietnam War was taking its toll, too. We kids couldn't ignore it because every boy, on his 18th birthday, got a letter from the Selective Service telling him when and where to report for his draft physical. (The draft lottery did not begin until the end of 1969.) The year I graduated from high school more than 300,000 Americans were serving in Southeast Asia. Every month thousands more were drafted and sent off into combat. College attendance permitted a deferral, not yet recognized as a cruel two-tiered system favoring the haves over the have-nots. We were immersed in war. (I would meet my future husband protesting it.)

When I was in high school and college, everybody knew boys who'd gone to Southeast Asia. Everybody. We didn't just talk about it; we watched news reports on TV every night. Everybody knew at least one boy who'd been killed or maimed. Everybody. A legendary varsity athlete in my graduating class, the object of countless crushes, chose the military instead of college. Within the year, he came back without a leg. Two years later, he was found dead of a drug overdose, in his car, parked at the local make-out spot above Lake Pearl.

As bad as things were in the world and in my family, I kept dancing. I'd stumbled upon the Sarazin School of Dance in No. Attleboro, a couple of miles from home, soon after we moved. A couple of my gymnastic/ dancing friends told me that it was the best place outside of Boston. They didn't lie. The Sarazin School, the place that saved me during my final years in high school! Not anything like most suburban strip mall dance schools, and I'm grateful for my time there.

The studio occupied a light-filled repurposed barn behind the Sarazin's home. It was a sacred space with the sounds of Stravinsky, Prokofiev, Tchaikovsky and others, issuing always from 78 r.p.m. recordings spun on a record player. That music signaled my entrance into the world of art and higher consciousness that I longed to enter. Mme. Sarazin was a strict but loving guide. She was so beautiful in her in black leotards and a black wrap skirt; her black hair pulled back into the *de rigeur* ballerina bun.[2]

My Saturday classes were a respite from my family but I was allowed to go only after I'd gone to mass and completed my chores. By then, I had to pay for my lessons myself, I was old enough, and to get myself to and from

---

2 A shout out to her exquisite daughter, my contemporary, the late Anamarie Sarazin, who was, for many years, a principal dancer with the Boston Ballet, renowned throughout the Northeast for her elegance and skill. Back at the school, a teenager, she was an alluring presence, often at the barre or on the floor in front of the mirrors, working on her pirouettes and fouettes.

my lessons. Undaunted, I walked several miles there and back, buoyed by my optimism and what I did not yet know was my resilience.

I showed up for my first private lesson with Mme. Sarazin with toe shoes in my bag, beautiful pink satin point shoes I'd saved up for and that I couldn't wait to dance in. I imagined myself performing *pas de bourree* on point, in a sparkling tutu and headpiece. That first day Mme. Sarazin told me, ever so kindly to put away my loved shoes. Sell them or give them away, she said. I wouldn't be needing them, that day or ever. I was too big and too old to train to become a ballerina, she explained. My feet weren't strong enough, she declared after examining them carefully with her slender fingers. I risked serious injury if I danced on point without the proper training. (At the time I was about 5'5" tall and I weighed about 120, a healthy weight for my height, but not for a dancer. In point shoes I'd be about 5'9".)

For the next two years, under Mme. Sarazin's disciplined but gentle tutelage, I worked on a balletic form of modern dance. Martha Graham and Isadora Duncan became icons even though I'd never seen them move, only their photographs. In my final year, we developed a Grahamesque dance to the mysterious lilting strains of L'Apres Midi D'une Faun, Claude Debussy's symphonic poem. I was thrilled with its choreography of leaps and twirls and falls. For the recital I performed barefoot, in a plain brown leotard, no sparkles or veils or frou-frou. Even so I was thrilled. I was moving toward my own amazing future even if it was not on point shoes as a ballerina. I almost fainted with happiness when Mme. Sarazin and her daughter told me how well I had done.

Something's Happening Here

S oon enough I graduated from King Philip with honors, but Daddy did not come to the ceremony. Ma took me, another of her chores. Daddy ignored my graduation, just as he'd ignored my final Sarazin performance of L'Apres Midi D'Un Faun. He'd already moved on to become superintendent of Newport Public Schools in Rhode Island. He left behind a swirl of conflicts among faculty and staff who either loved or loathed him. The heat of that anger and ambivalence buffeted me as I walked across the stage for my diploma.

The University of Massachusetts in Amherst was the school Daddy had chosen for me, not the school I wanted to go to. My first dream was to go to the brand new North Carolina School of the Arts, not yet part of the University of North Carolina system, to be a dance major. Daddy laughed. This idea was a non-starter because a school of the arts wasn't a real school and I wouldn't get a real education there, he said. I couldn't seriously pursue a career in dance. He laughed.

Instead, based on my overarching ambitions, and my artsy inclinations, he approved of my next two choices, Brown and Oberlin. Daddy agreed that, based on my stellar SATs and GPA, I should apply. The thought of attending those schools was an elixir my senior year. It blossomed into a beautiful fantasy (head still up there in the clouds.) I wouldn't have to worry about being smart, or maybe just a smart ass, a source of scorn at home. I'd flourish in one of those places, excelling at everything I tried. I'd graduate in glory and move on to the next amazing thing in my life.

This fantasy came back to me when I was watching Greta Gerwig's 2017 film Ladybird. The delightful title character dreamed obsessively of going to New York University, of escaping her dreary hometown of Sacramento. Her mother wanted her to stay home and commute to a local college. Against the wishes of his wife, Ladybird's father, played by Tracy Letts, mortgages the family home in order to make her dream come true. The moment rippled through me. I cried.

During my senior year I was wait-listed at Brown and I was certain, my entire senior year, that I'd make the cut. I just knew it!! I don't remember what happened with Oberlin. But when the time came to fill out the federal financial aid forms, and all the other necessary paperwork, Daddy, a skilled bait and switch artist, refused. He refused to fill out the parental paperwork for any school except the U Mass, a campus I'd never visited and had no desire to attend. I don't remember his reasoning, or the exact words he used to shatter my heart.

"You've got some nerve thinking you're good enough to go to one of those schools," he said or something like that. "Some nerve thinking you've earned it. You haven't."

This, then, was my punishment for my refusal to submit quietly to Daddy's tyranny: I would not be going to Brown or any other elite school. I got to go to the school he picked for me or not go at all.

Leaving Home

The day my parents drove me to Amherst to move me into my dorm was the first day I set foot on campus. U. Mass Amherst, a beautiful campus where I never got my bearings. Looking back from the distance of age, having raised three children, and taught in a public university for almost 30 years, I realize that, if I had somehow managed to excel at academics, for example, I might have found my own path and escaped Daddy's power once and for all. (This is how Elena Greco, the narrator of Elena Ferrante's incandescent Neopolitan Quartet of novels, makes her way out of her family and the bleak and violent neighborhood into which she had been born.) If only I could have found mentors to help me along the way, as, in the future, I would help many of my students. But that year I failed to take advantage of the opportunity to excel and escape. From the start I wandered the vast campus searching for, but never finding, a way to ground myself.

I lived in a new high-rise dorm but had trouble finding my way to my classes, the bookstore, the library, and the dining hall. I don't remember a single class I took, let alone any of my professors. I was a year younger than my peers, turning 18 in October after the semester started. Maybe my age and immaturity accounted for some of my problems. But I discovered that I had no idea how to take care of myself. Daddy had always taken care of everything. I couldn't deal with the administrative offices, financial aid or the registrar. I didn't know how to do the simplest bureaucratic task such as finding the registrar's office to complete a drop/add for the courses I wanted. I couldn't make phone calls. I was ashamed to ask anyone for help. I didn't know how to help myself. I was very afraid of anyone with authority, a plague that has continued through much of my life, and required intense cognitive behavioral therapy to partly overcome.

During my year at U.Mass, my father often wrote to me, what I now jokingly call poison pen letters. For decades I'd repressed the memory of them. My father, like his before him (Angus) was a skilled and confident writer. But in his letters to me, he wrote detailed analyses of my worthlessness and accountings of my many trespasses, concluding that I was un-deserving of his or anyone else's love. Also, it was costing him a 'small fortune,' he said, for me to live on campus, a privilege I didn't deserve and hadn't earned. (He'd spend another 'small fortune' to hide me in the home for unwed mothers.)

Daddy's letters created sinkholes I kept falling into but I understood this only in retrospect. I had repressed the memory of them until, in the writing of this story, I saw the letters there, their sickly glow, my father's distinctive handwriting, in the mail cubby in the lobby of the dorm. I still don't understand why I read them. At some point some of the girls on my floor advised me to stop – which had never occurred to me. (I know! I know!) After that, I dropped them into the trashcan near the cubbies. But his words had already seeped into me: I was unworthy of his or anyone else's love.

It's All Over Now

At U.Mass, I was a neophyte in the mechanics of romance. I didn't date in high school. I was too busy, too much of a dork, too uncertain of myself. (Nor did I get my driver's license. Driving and dating: too much potential for conflict in the family; more power struggles.) As I had in Bay Shore, in Plainville I mostly hung out in groups of girls. We considered ourselves rebels, but our biggest transgressions were smoking cigarettes and drinking too much coffee at the local diner while we planned our dazzling futures, our escape from dreary small town life.

Soon after I arrived in Amherst, one of my new friends introduced me to her boyfriend's best friend. Like her boyfriend, he was a freshman at Yale, a Jewish boy from Newton. We hit it off, this boy and I, two well-matched weirdos, gabbing for hours on end about music, politics, and the nascent counterculture.

He was my first, one of my very few, romantic relationships, but our relationship, the memory of it, was too painful to carry with me. I did not think of it as I sat in misery on my bed at St. Mary's, but only in my attempts to write a coherent story many decades later, trying to figure out the events leading up to my disaster. No doubt, at the time, I was trying to prove to myself that I was worthy of love in spite of my father's convictions. But because I did not remember these things in order, I struggled, at first, to connect them.

This boy – I'll call him David Rosen, not his real name, and not the father of my baby – had long hair; wore bottle thick eyeglasses for his extreme myopia, and dressed in somber military surplus clothing. His intelligence glistened in everything he said and did. He was serious, studious, an aspiring filmmaker whose family supported him in many ways I could neither see nor imagine. His minority status notwithstanding, he was comfortable in his own skin and in the world in a way that no one in my family would ever be. I was whatever I was, a dancer and a poet, an outlier in my religious, working class family, one obsessed with its arduous upward climb.

David and I connected in our shared quest to be on the cutting edge of everything. We were artists, determined to throw off the ancient patriarchal mores and march forward into the brave new world of equality, creativity and world peace! Yep, that's what we talked about. Our sincerity is laughable to me now, our belief that we could make the world a better place. I suppose we were ahead of the curve on that. Hippies and radicals hadn't yet taken over the culture, but we had our eye on them.

David and I were opposed to the war, to all wars, to military might, and authoritarian violence in all of its forms. Dylan was our bard, his lyrics inscribed deep into our consciousness but I can't use any of them here because of rigid copyright laws. Desolation Row, that one about selling post cards about the hanging, the blind commissioner, and the restless riot squad seems most relevant to our longings and perceptions.

Our connection was so deep I thought we were soul mates even if I did not yet know that term. But his was a wealthy, artsy family; worldly in a way I recognized but didn't understand. They wore their Judaism proudly even though they weren't observant. His grandparents and other family members had died during the Holocaust, one of the first things he told me about himself, and those who survived bore tattoos on their wrists.

Young as we were we understood our privilege. I should say David understood his privilege, but from the perspective of someone whose forbears had died during another war, while I understood that, as a female, I would not ever have to deal with it. Back then, college students could avoid the draft until they graduated from college. David's parents, like countless others, made certain he wouldn't have to serve – and an Ivy League education was as close to a guarantee as anyone could get.

I thought I loved him, a whole new thing for me. I had not experienced this kind of caring before and I suspect, in retrospect, that I didn't understand it or trust it. In some inchoate way, one I could not clearly see or explain, I thought we were made for each other.

Ma and Daddy loathed him from the instant they laid eyes on him. He embodied everything they feared about the changing culture, the very things I found irresistible. I figured that, at the very least, they'd recognize and respect his intelligence; his status as an Ivy League student; that he came from an accomplished, prosperous family. I hoped they'd be glad I found someone I wanted to be with. That they might respect my choice. But no. His long hair and military surplus clothing, not to mention his Judaism and prosperity, snuffed out that possibility. He was, plain and simple, a weirdo and they detested him. They could not abide the fact that I was a weirdo, too. That I'd placed myself on the fringes, believing life would be more meaningful there.

David drove down to Plainville over Thanksgiving to take me out. I was so excited: I had a boyfriend and we were going out! Where did not matter! My parents weren't exactly rude, but whatever the next worse thing was. I don't recall the details, only the discomfort of it. The next morning, unable to wait until I woke up, Daddy rousted me from bed to tell me David was a creep. "Why," he asked, "out of the thousands of guys at U. Mass, did you bring home this creep?" It was, he added, typical of my bad behavior. "I forbid you to see him again. He will never set foot in my house again."

As if my parents could stop me from seeing David while I was away in Amherst!

That day Daddy dragged me off to Confession so I could recite my trespasses to the priest breathing softly, silhouetted behind a screen in the lightless closet. What sins? I wondered. I didn't believe I had any. David and I had fooled around plenty but we hadn't yet gone "all the way." In the Confessional, I made things up. I lied. I got my absolution anyway. After that, I prayed my penance and my soul was cleansed.

David and I made a plan for New Year's Eve. I knew I was playing with fire but I didn't care. Nobody was going to keep me from seeing my one true love, the only person in the world who cared for me as I was, or so I believed. David planned to drive down from Newton to pick me up. I kept my plans to myself until that night because I knew it would trigger an explosion. Only at the last minute, did I tell Daddy and Ma. The expected eruption occurred, even crazier than I'd imagined.

Ma and Daddy blitzed me with name-calling. They no doubt hit me if I let them get into range, but by then I was smart enough to stay out of it. I kept thinking I'd be okay if I floated "like a butterfly," Mohammed Ali's infamous phrase from his fight with Cassius Clay.

"I'm going anyway, you can't stop me!" I shouted or something like that, words containing all the vitriol my 18-year-old self could muster. I simmered with rage. Any other life, no matter how precarious, would be better than the one I was living – I was sure of that. I'd rather die than keep living in Daddy's dictatorship. With my mother and my sister singing a chorus of tribulation. I don't remember most of what was said but soon enough, Daddy threw down the gauntlet: "If you leave with him tonight don't bother coming back."

We were fighting upstairs in the living room, a spotlighted geometric not unlike a boxing ring. My brothers and sisters would have been hiding in their bedrooms downstairs, maybe eavesdropping, maybe pretending they couldn't hear. The house thrummed with conflict. At last I went downstairs and packed my two suitcases, my worldly possessions. I carried them upstairs, then outside to the driveway. It was freezing with a crust of snow or ice on everything.

Already it was well past 9, our designated date time. No sign of David. No cell phones back then. No way to communicate. I stayed outside in the cold, waiting. And waiting. He'd show up any minute. I knew that. My life depended upon it. Two hours passed.

Ma and Daddy stayed in the living room, nothing better to do on New Year's Eve, taunting me from time to time. I stayed outside in the cold, holding onto my belief that David was on his way as if onto the very meaning of my life.

"You'll fall flat on your face," Daddy called out to me at one point or another, but I held my ground. "You'll come crawling back."

Around 11, David pulled into the driveway in his ancient BMW. I heard it rattling before I saw it. He was surprised to my suitcases in the driveway but he loaded them into his trunk without saying anything. And that was it. We left. My parents didn't come to the door. They did not say good-bye.

What could our plan for that night have been? To watch the Boston fireworks from some hidden outdoor spot he knew about? Smoke pot? Drink some Jack Daniels he'd taken from his parents' liquor cabinet? I don't remember the plan or what we ended up doing. Around 3 or 4 in the morning, we sneaked into his house, a place unlike any I'd ever seen, so beautiful. I lost my virginity on a teal silk couch in his living room, my blood staining it, likely ruining it. (Why the living room instead of his bedroom? I have no idea. Crazy kids.) David was still trying to clean this when his parents came back home. No memories of the scene that followed, only a vague recollection of David driving me to a Trailways station in Boston and waiting in gray light, the first day of 1966.

Desolation Row

When I arrived on campus, I got myself to student services, one of the first things I'd ever managed to do on my own. But I felt no triumph, only vulnerable and alone. Desperate. No triumph in my escape. Student services found me an empty dorm room in an unfamiliar building and gave me a pass for the only open dining room. Humiliated beyond belief, I spent the last two weeks of semester break by myself. I got to the library. I read a lot, but I don't remember what. I hung out in the almost empty cafeteria for a long time after every meal.

David and I talked by phone a couple of times, using a pay phone in the lobby of the dorm. I don't remember what we talked about. I don't remember what or how I felt about the loss of my virginity. I spent the two weeks trying to figure out my life but everything was so murky I couldn't figure out a thing. Alone in that strange dormitory room, the last threads of my resilience snapped, but I didn't realize this – or that my seemingly boundless optimism had deserted me. My pilot light flamed out. I turned numb to most everything. Now I understand that I was clinically depressed, in a crisis, but I did not see this when it was going on. Nobody else did either. Who would've seen? Who would have cared?

When I got back to my own dorm, another of Daddy's letters glowered in my cubby. I tossed it. His words already lived inside me and on my bad days they still do. A sense of injustice, one I wasn't able to articulate, blinded me. I was pulsing with unacknowledged anger.

After that, second semester was a blur of sadness and confusion. I don't remember any classes or much of anything else. Maybe I was punishing myself the way Daddy believed I should be punished. Or perhaps I was fulfilling his prophecies about my worthlessness.

(Years later one of my therapists described Daddy as cruel, possibly sadistic; that he got some satisfaction out of his carefully crafted verbal attacks on a daughter ill-equipped to fight back. I had trouble processing this idea. My entire life everybody outside the family and many in it told me how brilliant and how good he was; how lucky I was to be his daughter.)

Toward the end of second semester during my blurred period of hopelessness I met the father of my baby. I remember very little about him, not even how we met, a form of revenge, I suppose. Or maybe by then I'd split in two and I didn't understand the second me, a lost girl who didn't know she was in a crisis; who did not know how to protect herself; did not know that she was worth protecting.

I don't recall how or why we got together, or what he or our relationship meant to me. The relationship was more than a one-night stand, but less than a grand romance. I wasn't capable at the time, though I didn't know it, of having a much of a relationship with anyone. He was handsome, a fraternity bro, and I suppose that I, uncertain me, longing for love and validation, decided he was some kind of prize.

In the darkness of an alcohol-fueled night, with his arms around me, his desire enveloping me, maybe I felt a triumph of some sort. Maybe I wasn't loved, but I was desired. Maybe I couldn't tell those things apart. Whoever I might have been back then was locked away inside myself. I can't tell you what I was thinking about having unprotected sex because I don't know. I wasn't thinking.

I don't remember packing up my dorm room at U. Mass or leaving campus for the last time. I don't remember how I got home – my parents did not come for me – or anything else about what came right before or after that. I had no idea as I packed my books and bags that a little zygote had already settled into the warm welcoming flesh of my uterus. I hadn't occurred to me that I could be pregnant.

I dreaded going home but I had nowhere else to go. No money, no prospects, and no idea how to get them. No belief in my ability to make good decisions for myself, a plague that would follow me throughout my life. I wouldn't be returning to U. Mass, I'd made sure of that, but I couldn't come up with even a flimsy plan for my future. So back I went back to Plainville, an abject failure, fulfilling my father's prophecy that I'd 'come crawling back' to him.

I was not welcomed. My mother did not want me there any more than I wanted to be there. And Daddy made it clear to me that my acceptance "back into the family" was conditional, based solely on my good behavior. As long as I "toed the line" and obeyed the rules of the house, as long as I did not poison my brothers and sisters with my crazy ideas, I could stay. Daddy also forbade me, "for as long as you live in my house," to return to the Sarazin School. My parents had identified it as one source of my crazy ideas. No more dancing.

Toeing the line also meant not aggravating my mother, which was almost impossible because my mere presence aggravated her. She could barely tolerate the sight of me. And she had my sister Jane and my father in her corner. I had no one. I avoided my mother as best I could, not easy in that crowded little house. My other siblings and I hardly ever talked. My parents and I spoke to each other only when it could not be avoided. Every exchange, no matter how mundane, felt hostile, threatening. I was full of dread, a free-floating murk I couldn't begin to figure out. I was an abject failure, I knew that much. I was as worthless as my father had said, but I didn't yet understand that I was pregnant.

Early one morning, soon after I return home, my father bursts into my shared room and gathers up all of my books and papers and journals. He brings them to the burn can in the backyard and then comes back for all the other things I cherish most: a wide-brimmed hippie hat, some hand-made bracelets, dancing shoes and leotards, a macramé purse, who knows what else. He rifles through my bureau in the hallway and what serves as my closet. Once he is satisfied with the contents of the can, he squirts on lighter fluid and drops in a match. He stays there, gazing at the conflagration. I stay inside. I watch, paralyzed, the smoke rising up encircling his face. I choke on the smoky stench of my burning books and clothes. The stink stays with me all summer and sometimes I think I smell it at the home.

The Summer That Came Before

The summer of 1966 was a hallucinatory time, especially for those of us who lived with our heads in the clouds, our eyes on the horizon. The U.S. warplanes were bombing Hanoi and Haiphong. Nightly news featured dead American soldiers in body bags being unloaded from the bellies of hulking gray Air Force cargo planes, a grim ritual played out at Dover Air Force Base in Delaware. The bodies in those bags were our classmates, cousins, friends, and friends of friends. And I felt, even if I couldn't articulate the idea, that I'd already lost everything worth having. I could not see a future for myself.

As per usual, Daddy found me a job on the line at a nearby factory. This one manufactured high-end Catholic iconography, rosary beads and medals and crucifixes, items fashioned of gold, silver, and semi-precious stones. A friend of his ran the place. All day I glued satin inserts into snap-shut velvet boxes that would hold the shimmering rosary beads. We workers punched a time clock and got paid in cash at the end of the week. Our pay came in tiny manila envelopes with a tally of our days and hours stamped on the back. On Fridays I handed Daddy my weekly pay envelope to work off my college debt. He would not let me keep an allowance for the books and magazines I loved. "Go to the library," he said.

The days of the hot summer tick slowly past, endless days of solitary anguish. I sit at a long table with older women, substantial mothers and grandmothers, heavy smokers all. They like me; they like to tease me and joke and wonder what a nice girl like me is doing in a place like that. They encourage me to complete my education so that I don't end up like them. I sit amid the swirling smoke and women's chatter, with multiple radios tuned to different stations, a cacophony of news and Top 40 hits. All day I sit gluing the satin inserts into the velvet boxes that snapped shut. Sometimes I burned a finger with the hot glue, or accidentally shut the box on one. Nine hours a day, five days a week with an hour off for lunch.

At lunchtime we swarm out to food trucks parked outside. We eat greasy burgers and grinders and fries, and drink bottled Coca Cola. We eat at picnic tables on the factory's grounds, no shade but still fresh air. Then we go back onto the line for four more hours. Industrial fans create a steady hum but only whiffs of cooler air.

My head stayed in the clouds. I did not learn, as my father had hoped I would, to live in the real world. Even the women I worked with cautioned me in many different ways: "Get out as soon as you can and don't come back." I missed at least three periods before I began to understand that I must be pregnant, a possibility that, despite my sexual relationship with the baby's father, had not occurred to me.

Rather I seemed to be fighting off a chronic low-grade nausea, and I vowed to myself that I'd never ever again do factory work. But as the weeks passed, my body, the one with which I had hardly any connection, began to speak loudly, an alarm ringing all through me. Sore swollen breasts. No period. No fucking period. I checked my underpants every time I peed, hoping, hoping, and hoping that a red stain would appear. It never did. I had the presence of mind to take menstrual pads from the gigantic communal box in the bathroom closet at home and then I trashed them in wastebaskets at work. That way my mother and sister wouldn't know I'd stopped menstruating. And then I felt the baby move.

Feeling the baby move, the quickening.

That's when reality cut me with its terrible serrated edge. But a fierce love also ignited within me, an internal tsunami, the overwhelming desire to protect the child I carried at all costs, a feeling that got deeper and deeper as my pregnancy went on. It complicated everything.

Baby Daddy

I knew what town the baby's father lived in but I didn't have his home phone number or he mine – that's how close we were. Still I had to find him. I had to tell him, once I confirmed my status to myself, that I was pregnant. I don't know what I wanted from him; what, if anything, I was hoping for. Even so I felt that I had to. I was desperate to do so when an acquaintance from high school, a friend of a friend of a friend, told me about a party that was going to happen at Craigville Beach on Cape Cod. The father of my baby would be there with his buddies. No idea how this distant friend had acquired his intel. No idea how I got to the beach or back home, but I did.

A bonfire. A swarming college party, scores of kids, the kind of gathering I'll never again be part of. I seek him, the guy with whom I had been fooling around that spring. Sex was the only thing we had in common but I couldn't see that at the time. I thought he cared about me. But here now, on the beach, he's not glad to see me. Nevertheless, I lead him to a more private spot.

"I'm pregnant," I tell him, straight out, otherwise I would've lost my nerve. "I'm going to have a baby." He's quiet for a moment. Then he laughs. "Not mine," he says. and he rambles on that the baby couldn't possibly be his because he was, after all, the world's greatest expert at withdrawal. He had never ejaculated inside of me. He is certain of this fact. "Could be anybody's," he repeats though I don't remember his words. The baby could be anybody's. He shakes his head, still laughing, as if I'm a comedian who's just told a terrific joke.

He's having a good time, this guy who has also left the university, who plans to enlist, or maybe by then he already had. He isn't interested in anything else I have to say and I don't have the nerve to argue. He has been done with me for some time. He never thought about me again after the semester was over. Why am I ruining his night? He disappears back into the crowd, the hot summer night, the flames of the bonfire shooting upward.

I don't bother going after him. He walks back to his buddies, telling them what I'd just told him. Bragging. Soon the gossip will burn through wide swaths of classmates, neighbors, family, and friends. If I could have I would have jumped into the flames.

After that encounter I cut him out of my memories. I cut him out the same way some girls cut a guy's images from photographs after they've broken up. I cut him out completely. I never saw him or heard from him again and I didn't want to. For the duration of my pregnancy and everything that happened afterward mine might as well have been an immaculate conception. That's how much he had to do with it. I never told anyone his name, except his son half a century later. My mother is the only person who ever asked. I told her I didn't know, just to get her goat. She smacked me.

Spinning Round And Round

I had trouble telling my parents anything about myself beyond my grades and alleged sins. Nothing else mattered. That's how our family worked. Maybe they were overwhelmed, or distracted, or just not interested. I couldn't tell them when I was sad or when I had a headache or a stomachache. How could I tell them I was pregnant? I could not imagine doing it. I could not think of anyone who might help me. I did not want *my friends to realize that I'd gotten caught, one of the uncoolest things that* could happen to anyone in the 60s. Shame was already knitting a sturdy shawl around me but it chilled instead of warming me. I put off telling Ma and Daddy until I could see my own swelling belly, when all of my clothes were too small and I had no money to get new ones.

I left a short note, sealed in an envelope, on my mother's bureau. The detonation occurred when I get home from work at the rosary bead factory. It happened behind closed doors in my parents' bedroom, a foreign land. Daddy was waiting for me too.

My revelation to my parents was so explosive that no rational discussion of my pregnancy or of the baby's future was possible. I suppose they knocked me around, physically and verbally, but the details of that long ago brawl have shrunk into the dark place and I'm content to leave them there.

The day I told my parents I was pregnant was a pivot point: the day the secret passed from me to them and took hold, with its clawed grip, of our lives. The rest of our lives. That moment was a shattering. In its wake I lost whatever little control I'd had over my own life.

Today Daddy takes me to see the pastor of our parish, St. Martha's in Plainville. (St. Martha is the sister of Lazarus, the woman who witnessed Jesus raising him from the dead.) Our pastor, a monsignor, also serves as Daddy's confessor. He sees my father as pious, almost saintly, the perfect Catholic.

We meet in a small shadowy room of the rectory, its walls adorned with portraits of the saints. He wears a floor-length black cassock trimmed with magenta. A purple sash encircles his big waist. His vestments tell me that very serious business is afoot. His face above his clerical collar is pink and puffy. His name is that of a popular fish, a fish born in freshwater that migrates to salt water and returns to fresh water to spawn. As I look at him, about to leave my body and float nearby, I think about this fish, served often for our meatless Friday suppers, its tireless migrations.

I cannot focus on the good monsignor's words. They have to do with the forgiveness of sins, the saving of my soul, the path to salvation and life ever-lasting. This may be when I'm supposed to confess my sins, mortal sins, and do penance in order to achieve salvation. But I don't remember if I do. I'm supposed to ask for forgiveness, but I don't remember if I do. I remain mute, scalded by humiliation and rage. I look at his florid face, his shiny eyeglasses. His words, a soft breeze, waft past me signifying nothing.

The day Daddy took me to the rectory of St. Martha's parish to meet with the monsignor was a humiliation so profound I turned mute. I couldn't breathe. But it turned out to be just the first of countless encounters I would have in the coming weeks and months with official adults: nuns and clergy, and counselors and caseworkers, so-called adoption professionals. They were representatives of an adoption industry (the unholy trinity) that I did not yet know existed.

Every one of them was focused on my transgressions, my delinquency, my sins, and I shriveled in their presence. All were eager advocates of secret newborn adoption, the only possible path out of my mess. They were going to fix me and save me, if only I would allow them to.

Redemption was a key word. Salvation. Deliverance. Atonement was never mentioned but its inescapable variations would soon take over my life.

As I've pieced it together, my father and the monsignor sought help from Catholic Charities of the Archdiocese of Greater Boston. This was, unknown to me, the go-to family services (a.k.a. adoption) agency for girls like me. Soon I'd be assigned a caseworker, Gail Kirker Murray, a childless true believer. She'd usher me through my ordeal, acting as my new best friend, until I signed the termination of parental rights documents, of which I have no memory. After that she wouldn't answer my calls or letters.

Not one of these grown-ups (as I thought of them back then) ever asked me what I wanted. From the start it was clear that what I wanted did not matter. I was not allowed to want. It was a given that I'd surrender my baby immediately after his or her birth and keep the secret ever after. That I would immediately forget about the misbegotten child and go on with my life. I would forget, they insisted, and I believed them. I clung to their promises as to a tether that might save me from drowning. That might, if I held on tightly enough, offer me a chance at a new start once my ordeal was over.

Back then, at the beginning, I had no opinion on the matter of signing away my parental rights. I was too numb, too overwhelmed, too frightened and ashamed, for an opinion. No one in this legally regulated process ever explained my rights to me or offered any alternative. Not a single word. Nor did anyone offer a scintilla of empathy. Yes, at 18, I was officially an adult but I didn't think of myself that way. I'd never had any adult privileges, no earned freedoms. I didn't have a driver's license or a bank account. I had no idea how to stick up for myself. Maybe I was, emotionally, still 15.

I remained desperate for affection, for understanding and respect, but almost immediately I grasped that the adults of the unholy trinity, oh so concerned about my future, weren't actually interested in me at all. No, the so-called adoption professionals did not care who I really was or the particulars of how I'd gotten into my dilemma. They didn't give a whit about the baby's father, or any claims he might have on our child. Which, at the time, was fine by me. I had deleted him as completely as possible from my life. He no longer existed for me. The adoption professionals didn't notice or didn't care. That may be when I began to see shadowy images of myself as a prisoner in an amorphous system that I didn't understand and couldn't fight. Yet it never occurred to me to wonder if my rights were being violated. Never. It did not occur to me that I had rights. I was forlorn and frightened and confused, a goat sent out into the wilderness.

PART THREE

Choose Oblivion

The social historian Rickie Solinger, in her landmark 1993 study, *Wake Up Little Susie: Single Pregnancy and Race Before Roe V. Wade,* offers a sharp-eyed view of the post-war phenomenon of mass closed adoption. Her analysis traces how, beginning in the pre-WWII years, those in power manipulated and coerced unmarried pregnant (white) females into giving up their babies, and then shamed them into silence. As far as I can tell, Solinger's is the first cogent analysis of closed adoption.

Solinger describes, as if she'd visited St. Mary's: "The world of maternity homes in postwar America was a gothic attic obscured from the community by the closed curtains of gentility and high spiked fences. The girls and women sent inside were dream-walkers serving time, pregnant dream-walkers taking the cure. Part criminal, part patient, the unwed mother arrived on the doorstep with her valise and, moving inside, found herself enclosed in an idea."

The "idea" Solinger speaks of was that unmarried pregnant girls were "not mothers." Everyone with power (parents, clergy, adoption agencies, family courts) agreed by then that unmarried pregnant females, no matter their ages, were rather, as demonstrated by their pregnancies, pathological and unfit to parent their own children. We were a danger to them. This idea took hold in the pre-WWII years of the 20th century and developed ever more sturdily, encountering few obstacles, after the war. It billowed like a mushroom cloud until the late '60s sexual revolution, made possible by the availability of The Pill, and the passage of the recently overturned Roe V. Wade in 1973.

Among emerging social workers, with their Psychology 101 backgrounds, and pious motivations, it was an article of faith that unmarried pregnant girls and women had gotten knocked up on purpose – as a demented way to thwart her family. Engaging in unmarried sex became the litmus test for sanity versus pathology. This theory turned the unwed mother into a crazy person, a danger to her own offspring. This concept of unmarried mother as threat not only went unchallenged during those decades but was quickly accepted by wide swaths of the population, determined to keep young women chaste and submissive.

Rather than being tossed away as a revolting delinquent, lost forever in the dungeon of the culture, she required rescue, rehabilitation, therapy, and redemption. None of these could be achieved if she kept her baby, if the world knew of her transgression. The do-gooders, like their forebears in the red light districts, sprang into action.

This explains, at least partly, why by mid-century onward, shelters for unmarried pregnant females became places of dark secrets and sequestration. More and more bastard babies were born to never married mothers and handed over (with changed birth certificates) to married couples. However, no federally mandated record keeping existed; only flimsy state laws that no one paid much attention to. Birth records, in particular, were falsified, often even the originals, redacting the names of the scandalous birth mother and father. Those false but legal amended birth certificates accompanied countless infants into their new homes while family courts sealed the originals. Adopted children grew up none the wiser until or unless their new parents decided to tell them.

Consequently, over the course of many mid-century years, while bastard babies were transfigured (rebranded!) into blue ribbon babies, and prosperous infertile white couples endorsed their own entitlement to children who looked like them, more than a million very young women, pregnant and unmarried, me included, languished in the strange confinement of maternity homes (the Republic of Shame) knowing nothing.

The year I gave up my son, more than 85,000 other unmarried American girls did the same. By 1970, the University of Oregon's Adoption Research Project states that the number had ballooned to 170,000, doubling in just three years! The majority of these adoptions were brokered by social workers employed by adoption agencies and religious homes for unwed mothers. Money, lots of it, changed hands. It still changes hands. Somewhere in the shadows, closed adoption became a big business for so-called nonprofits with their many well-paid administers. Their major, though never-stated, task was seeking ways to proliferate themselves. It remains so today. Think, Adoption Industrial Complex.

According to various Internet sources, it now costs about $50,000 to adopt a healthy white or white-ish newborn. I don't know how much it cost back then. No doubt it was proportionally similar. And all the while we sad girls stayed hidden, unknowing, awaiting the births and relinquishment of our babies, and our own salvation, an experience from which most of us would never recover.

We degenerate girls were confined in the so-called homes to be rehabilitated, cured of our sinful ways, our bad behaviors. Redemption and rehabilitation were the interwoven goals of our sequestrations. We had to be made ready for our reentrance into the real world, our babies gone, yes, but our salvation in the works.

According to researchers, this rehabilitation, or transformation or salvation or any of the other words they used to create a positive spin on their machinations, involved a step-by-step process overseen by the new crop of social workers eager to demonstrate their diagnostic skills, and their ability to fix the lives of those of us who'd chosen the wrong path. Hence, after my meeting with the good monsignor, and my acceptance into the asylum, I had frequent sessions with a therapist, a social worker, or a psychologist, I'm not sure what her credentials were. I remember her name but because she is still living, I'll rename her Jackie. I also met frequently with my caseworker.

Jackie was glamorous, sleek and shiny amid the nuns in their habits and the social workers in their prim dark clothes. Sophisticated, or whatever my idea of sophisticated was at that age. Patterned sheathe dresses in lovely fabrics, most definitely not homemade, like my clothes. Maybe a blazer or a silk cardigan. Pumps and stockings. Nude stockings, a faint shimmer on her calves. Always pumps and I envied them, soft leather, slender heels. She wore earrings, bracelets, necklaces. Not too showy, but always evident. Short hair, red and feathery, freckles. I think, thought, she might have been gay, closeted, because such an orientation was, at that time, still a crime.

Our talks were a break from the tedium of life in confinement, a chance to see whatever she was wearing that day, and a chance to vent, mostly grievances about my parents and the dreadful food. Jackie was a bright, lively conversationalist. I trusted her as much as I trusted anyone at that time. For reasons I can't explain, I thought she was on my side even though she was among those who convinced me that I did not have the right to become a mother. (*The most loving thing you can do for your baby is to give it to parents with the means to raise it well as you could never do. Your baby will be better off without you.*)

I'm not positive that either she or my caseworker ever said these exact words, but these are the words that live inside me.

I believed that our sessions were confidential, just between us. Maybe I told Jackie things I shouldn't have, even though I suspected she was in touch with my parents. Perhaps she thought they were her clients since they were paying for her services. I had no idea what her strategies were. I would not find out until after I'd reconnected with my son a half a century into the future.

There's so much that I, a sad lonely girl, didn't understand. But I always understood one important thing: I was not entitled to an opinion about much of anything, and most especially, not about giving up my baby. I didn't understand that I had a legal right to say "no" to the surrender of my child. I don't remember anyone ever telling me I did. I don't remember anyone ever asking me, and certainly not Jackie or my caseworker. Instead, in these counseling sessions, they offered a Dickensian vision of the abyss I'd fall into if I kept my baby: we'd be lost in the world, homeless, shunned everywhere, with neither a penny of support nor a scrap of affection from anyone.

They, the grown-ups, reminded me time and again that I had no money and no way to get any. (No getaway car.) I didn't know anything about social service programs like welfare, and no one in the unholy trinity ever shared such information. Not a word. Not ever. What I understood, in a vague way not to be examined, was that I didn't have the right to become a mother.

Brainwashing was a newish idea in Sixties popular culture. The term was first used in the '50s, during the Korean War, to describe how the Chinese government got soldiers to cooperate in plans that violated their deepest beliefs about themselves. By the time I got to St. Mary's, the nuns and priests and counselors and caseworkers and even my own parents were skilled in its strategies. I remember very little about my so-called therapy sessions, and even less about my meetings with my caseworker, but I know that my identity, my nub of a self, was smashed to bits in them. My acceptance of impending motherhood and my nascent desire to parent my child were turned inside out. Instead, my feelings about myself, my sense of unworthiness and self-loathing, took hold during those sessions. They've lingered inside me ever since, ghostly and malignant.

Degenerate, depraved, defiled, debauched.

Were such words ever actually used during our sessions? I cannot say for sure – but even if unspoken these words floated in the air we breathed, penetrating my fragile innermost self. I've yet to find another birth mother, and I've talked to dozens through my membership in Concerned United Birthparents and attending its support groups and retreats, who emerged from these "counseling" sessions with a positive sense of herself.

These sessions prior to the birth were part of the step-by-step process of my redemption. In them, I was counseled, encouraged, to get knocked out with anesthesia during labor so I wouldn't remember anything about the birth or the actual handing over of my newborn.

Everything would be so much easier, I was told, if I were unconscious during the key parts of birth and relinquishment. Many girls chose these options and would, later in life, be haunted by their choices. So would the fathers of their babies who were left with nothing to go on when they searched for their lost children. Commercial DNA databases, for those who use them, have provided some answers to the questions in these broken families. I learned of this appalling reality in my support groups for birth parents, when members told their stories.

No matter how many times these "no contact" suggestions were repeated to me, I said no. I wanted to be conscious during the birth (a decision I would question when I was in the midst of labor.) During these sessions, I told anyone who'd listen, that, after the birth, I wanted see and hold and feed my baby, to care for him in whatever way was allowed for as long as I could. I'm not sure why I was so adamant in the face of opposition except that, by then I felt a crazy love for the baby I was carrying. It was a love I'd never before experienced, though it never occurred to me that I might have the right to keep my baby. Both my counselor and caseworker, allowing me a tiny bit of agency, agreed to this plan.

I question now, though I didn't then, what I learned in those all-important rehab sessions, what I came away with. That I was going to give my baby to decent people, worthy people, a mother and a father with the means to give the baby everything they'd need to get through life. Which I could never ever do. Obviously. Because I was bad, so flawed, that my baby would be better off without me. And anyway, I'd soon forget all about him. (Forgetting, the essential promise of the Baby Scoop.)

But as the days and weeks and months of pregnancy went on, as I rubbed my belly and loved my gestating baby (gender as yet unknown), a notion thrashed and throbbed inside me. I could feel it even if I could not see it, an awareness I was not allowed to have, that I was serving as a breeder for people far more powerful than myself.

Me In My Body

Before I arrived at St. Mary's, I knew I'd be having my prenatal care and delivering my baby at St. Margaret's Hospital Lying in Hospital, which shared an urban campus with the asylum. St. Margaret's, geared toward female health care, was considered highly prestigious. Those of us sequestered at the asylum could walk across the campus to the clinic for our appointments. While the counselors and caseworkers attended to my mind, my spiritual rehabilitation, St. Margaret's health care providers tended to my body.

I didn't know what prenatal care involved when I got pregnant. Nobody had ever told me and I never asked anyone. Hence, pregnancy introduced me, in stunning ways, to the reality of my own body. Growing up, I was so out of touch with it that I hardly ever knew when I was tired or hungry or thirsty, sad or happy, hot or cold. When I felt a sexual desire. I was a stranger to myself. Often, when I was growing up, I felt disembodied. Sometimes I still do.

Neither gossip nor old wives tales prepared me for my first pelvic examination in St. Margaret's clinic. Neither my friends nor my sister had ever had one. Or, if they had, they remained silent about it. Not until my feet were placed into those cold metal stirrups for the first time, did I realize what was going to happen. Not just that once, but, after that, over and over again until my child was born.

Until it happened, I didn't understand that my warm soft body, its flesh and muscles and blood and fluids and orifices, the zygote it contained, would become the site of countless never-explained probings, palpations, intrusions with metal instruments and the gloved fingers of many strangers.

I failed to comprehend the grim details of what happened to powerless teenage girls back then (no partners, no advocates) in teaching clinics. Nobody explained. Maybe my parents didn't understand either, or maybe they just didn't care. The white-coated interns, clip boards in hand, gathered round to watch while the patient's breasts are bared, her vagina cranked open, its flesh and fluids touched, pointed out, discussed. Prenatal care as a form of assault. That's how it felt to me. But I never said a word about this to Jackie or to anyone else. I couldn't express my feelings even though they would impinge upon my prenatal care with my other babies, that implicit memory of violation. I knew they'd ignore my complaints or refuse to listen.

Not until the mid-1970s did the concept of "informed consent" begin to impact how medical professionals treated their patients. Informed consent: a patient's right to know what is being done to her and why and her right to accept or refuse said treatment. No such concept in the treatment of the unmarried mothers of the Baby Scoop. During childbirth, I was given an episiotomy that took almost a month to heal. Nobody asked and nobody told. I found out only when I complained to a nurse about the pain and she told me how to go the bathroom and to use a sitz bath to ease the discomfort.

From the start, my treatment felt wrong, so wrong, but I could not do anything about it. After my check-ups I'd go back to St. Mary's, crawl into my cot in a room with no privacy, put a pillow over my head, and cry until I couldn't anymore.

During my prenatal care, I began to realize how little control I had over my own body. This realization was soon swamped by another: I'd never had much control over my own body. I'd never felt ownership over it. And every encounter with the nurses and doctors triggered what I would have, if I could have, described as despair.

Maybe this is what happens when you're raised in a family like mine in which the body is a mere carrying case for the eternal soul, and a shameful one at that. When those with power over it, mothers and fathers, feel free to smack it, shove it, ridicule it and deprive it of affection and tenderness.

Not for another decade, as the result of the first wave of feminism, would the term bodily autonomy, the basis of informed consent, enter public discourse. It has remained firmly planted there ever since. Bodily autonomy, like the right to an accurate birth registration, is now considered a basic human right. Any unpermitted intrusion upon it is considered a human rights violation. This concept has changed, quite dramatically classroom behaviors, medical treatments and many other facets of daily life. But the unholy trinity and the many thousands in their employ, remained ignorant of anything like bodily integrity or informed consent. Or if they knew of it, they ignored it. They did whatever they decided to do to the young women in their care. They functioned as if they held by divine right, sovereignty over the bodies of the pregnant females under their control. Millions of them.

Despite my cluelessness during my time at the "home," I figured that everything would get worse before it got better. After all, I hadn't yet birthed my child. With almost no agency over my body and none over my future, I began to feel not quite human, with no thoughts or feelings worth considering. A pawn. Yet my sense, however vague, of manipulation and abuse was not always shared by the other girls. Many were sincere penitents, begging forgiveness at every turn. But I couldn't rid myself of that uneasy feeling about the wrongness of it all, one I couldn't yet explain: that I was being played by hands I couldn't see and over which I had no power.

I did not know and would not learn for half a century that the kind of treatment I received was typical, an accepted part of the plan that hardly anyone acknowledged: an intricate and efficient state-sanctioned system that was geared toward taking away our babies and giving them to someone else.

Only decades later, following numerous studies by social scientists, was this period named the Baby Scoop. By then those same researchers recognized it as an ad hoc experiment in social engineering: taking offspring from "unworthy" unmarried parents and handing them off to prosperous infertile married couples. By then a wealth of other research documented the lifelong consequences suffered by a baby abruptly taken from its mother following birth. Not long afterward, in the 1990s, research confirmed a similar emotional cost to the mother following this same abrupt separation. Both revealed that this separation has lifelong repercussions for both mother and child.

For me, and no doubt many others, this experience was a breaking wheel, one whose overseers refused to acknowledge its existence, let alone its cruelty. From the moment I told my parents I was pregnant, I was bound to it, like Captain Ahab to the white whale, but I didn't know anything about it. That wheel rolled onward toward the cataclysmic changes of the 70s, when it screeched to a halt – against the now demolished bulwark of safe and legal abortion, and safe available female contraception.

Mother Love

Throughout my stay at the asylum I thrummed with envy when the mothers of the other girls showed up. I couldn't help but see them coming and going, the girls and their mothers. I heard them chattering on the pay phones in the halls. Not me. Ma was missing in action. Then one day Jackie told me that my mother was coming to take me out to lunch! This was a huge surprise! No visits, phone calls or letters since I'd arrived. Jackie's delight notwithstanding, I dreaded my mother's visit even as I felt flicker of hope that she might offer me a bit of understanding or empathy.

I meet Ma on the sidewalk outside St. Mary's. She drives me to a luncheonette in nearby Upham's Corner. I'm as nervous as if I'm with a stranger but my mother's worse, even more jittery and hyper-alert to everyone and everything around us. What if we run into somebody we know? What if the secret gets out? She cannot look at me. She looks past me or above my face, never at my belly.

Ma's 39 but looks younger. She's a pretty and petite brunette with a sweet smile and green eyes that I inherited from her. I'm disoriented to be doing something alone with my mother. I can count on one hand the number of times she and I have been alone together. Someone else seemed always to interfere. I had to get past others to reach her. Now, across from each other at a small table in a crowded steamy restaurant in the middle of the city, it's just the two of us. We order platters of fried clam strips with cole slaw and French fries. Cokes to drink. This is a big splurge. We never ate out in my family. And compared to what they feed us at the home, this is a feast of salt and grease. Amazing! I'm ravenous but soon realize it's not for something on our plates.

We eat. We don't talk. (What could we have talked about?) Ma does not ask me anything. She does not want to know anything.

Our lunches include a desert of chocolate pudding with a swirl of whipped cream on top. I'm digging into mine when Ma finally speaks. "You are a terrible, terrible girl," she says. I look up at her, but she's still looking past me. "What's wrong with you? Why can't you be like your sisters?"

I have five of them, sisters. Not to mention two brothers. I go back to eating my pudding.

"I don't understand it, your terrible behavior, with all the love you have been given, all the opportunities you've had."

I would've eaten my mother's pudding, too, if she offered it, but she doesn't. She'd never had any advantages herself, not like the ones I'd had, she says as she licks her spoon. After all, she was an orphan. She'd been farmed out to whatever relatives would take her.

The waitress comes with the bill. Ma pays it. She drives me back to the home. She doesn't park. She doesn't wait until I run inside. She leaves me with a question I haven't yet been able to answer with any certainty: "How could you do this to us?"

"With all the love you have been given." This statement swirled in my teenage mind when I got back to the home and for days afterward. With all the love you have been given. I couldn't process it. My mother and I must have had very different concepts of love because I did not feel loved. I'd never felt loved by my mother. During our next session I told Jackie lunch with Ma was a disaster. "I don't think she loves me," I said. Jackie frowned and sighed. "I was hoping you could work out your differences, at least some of them, before the baby's born," she said. That's when I realized she'd arranged our lunch date. My mother had been prodded or embarrassed into taking me out.

"You're bearing her first grandchild," Jackie said, not meeting my eyes, "whether she likes it or not. She has a responsibility to you."

Ironically, perhaps, the session with Jackie I remember most concerned the concept of "mother love," not a mother's love, but mother love. Mother love, a felt thing, difficult or perhaps impossible to describe, especially for this counselor who had no children of her own. I doubted that my own mother had ever felt it with me, maybe not with any of us.

Mother love was, as Jackie tried to describe it, a profound connection, one that happened in the body between a mother and her fetus. During the 40 weeks of gestation. Maybe it's what we call "bonding" today, a term that didn't come into usage until the 70s and then became of overarching importance in the 2010s and 2020s when my daughters gave birth, soon after one another.

Of course, I felt "mother love" though I didn't have a name for it when it happened: a potent vapor that swept through me the moment I felt my baby move, a fluttering, a strange sensation, an all-encompassing thrill. My baby moving! It had happened on the line in the rosary bead factory and triggered the deepest love I'd ever experienced even as it terrified me. The feeling warmed and buoyed me. It gave me the courage to go on, and helped me through the many discomforts of my pregnancy. From then on, I was possessive, protective and I also felt vulnerable, and under constant threat. At night, in bed, I cried a lot.

But I did not tell Jackie about my feeling of mother love. I could not let Jackie or anyone else to know how vulnerable and scared mother love was making me feel. Maybe she was assuming, or hoping, that I didn't feel mother love, and, from her perspective, it was perfectly fine if I did not. As in, "You might or might not feel mother love. Either way is fine." Or, "Do you think you feel mother love?" (Jotting in her notebook.) "Of course, it's

OK if you don't. Some don't feel it until late in the pregnancy. And some never feel it at all."

In fact, though Jackie never said this, I knew it would be better for everyone involved if I, along with the legions of other unmarried and very young pregnant women, did not feel mother love. If we did not bond with our babies and if they did not attach to us. Without ever saying it, the toilers of the unholy trinity discouraged "mother love" and did what they could to prevent it, mostly undermining our sense of self to the point that we could not imagine such a thing. Mother love! (Not available to us sinful girls.) That way, the ones controlling the narrative could feel comfortable in their insistence that our babies were "unwanted," among the most enduring and destructive of all the adoption myths. It's what my surrendered son grew up believing, that I had not wanted him, a belief that undermined from our first meeting our ability to connect.

Ghost Mother

My mother, thirty years after her death, still haunts me. I dream about her, hear her calling to me. She wakes me up and talks to me in a way she never did in life. I write about her over and over again, a seemingly endless profusion of ambiguous mother-daughter stories, not to mention an entire novel, *Mimi Malloy, At Last!,* her fictional biography. Still, she won't leave me alone.

You'd think she'd have better things to do. She was, after all, the mother of eight children all of whom have married and all but one have reproduced. You'd think she'd spend some time haunting them. She doesn't. I've checked.

But then, it's possible that the rest of my siblings had worked out all of their shit with her. Or maybe they did not believe they had shit to work out. Maybe they'd said everything that needed to be said before she died, at 64, of a massive stroke. Maybe they were more forgiving, less needy. Maybe her mothering didn't leave them feeling bereft the way it left me.

The haunting occurred after her death, never back when I was confined to the unwed mothers home. Back then our relationship was a profound and painful mystery, one I couldn't begin to figure out. I tried to never think about it.

My mother, as far as I could tell, endorsed enthusiastically the postwar ideal of the happy and well-turned-out stay-at-home mother who lived to serve her husband. As promoted in glossy women's magazines, Ma aspired to create a meticulously clean and well-organized home for her husband and children. She never had money to spend but she nevertheless made sure we all met high standards. (We were lace curtain, not shanty!) But with Daddy constantly interfering and undermining her efforts, he berated her as often as he did us, this was a reach always beyond her grasp.

In many ways, at least as I see it now, my mother was as much a victim of cultural and religious norms as I was. Her entire life, a hard one from the start, my mother submitted to the master plot of Catholic dogma: submission to the will of the head of household and the strictures against contraception. Sexual love in marriage had a singular purpose: the propagation of the faith.

I'm not convinced that Ma enjoyed being a mother, a fact she could not ever admit to anyone, not even to herself. Or maybe, as the second of her eight children, I just did not see her pleasure in mothering, never felt it. I don't know if she experienced 'mother love.' How could she have had time to feel such a thing? Or maybe my mother kept her pleasure in mothering strictly to herself. Who could blame her? Not I. I knew as soon as I knew anything, that my mother was overwhelmed and full of secrets and Daddy was oblivious. From my perspective, she had very little control over her own life. I never wanted a life like hers, something I knew by the time I was in first grade. She didn't even get to buy the groceries or plan menus, only cook them. Daddy did the shopping and planning and railed about her imperfections as a cook.

Ma never shared a birthing story with any of us, narratives that are today a staple of mommy blogs and family stories. *On the day you were born...*(My daughters tell and retell their birthing stories, just as I've done with mine, except for the first.) At least six of us, maybe all of us, were born with my mother under "twilight sleep." That combination of morphine and scopolamine was designed to reduce the pain of childbirth and alleviate the memory of it. My mother never talked about our births but perhaps behind the morphine and scopolamine, she had no stories to tell. Perhaps, steeped in faith-based and familial reticence, she didn't understand the mechanics herself. Unlike many contemporary mothers, she might not ever have experienced joy or wonder in her childbearing. If she did, she never let on.

For my 40th birthday, my father sent me a birthday card containing some handwritten pages from a yellow legal pad, his favorite paper. By then he'd "adjusted" his letter writing tactics though I was still fearful of opening that envelope. (His handwriting on the front was enough to trigger me.) In the birthday card, he told me that my birth, in a tiny hospital in northern Maine, had been held back. According to his story, the doctor wasn't there when I began crowning. Two nurses, he said, climbed onto the bed and held my mother's legs together for an unknown period of time (15 minutes? Half an hour?) until the doctor showed up. My mother was under anesthesia, most likely twilight sleep, when I was born blue and rushed off, in a car driven by my father, to a larger hospital with the ability to handle a distressed newborn. By some twist of fate I survived without brain damage. I was returned to my mother after almost a week. My mother was still hospitalized. As I understand it, she was healing from the bruising she experienced as I tried to heave myself into the world. In Daddy's version of the story, Mother and Child lived happily ever after. In my version of the story, my mother and I never bonded after the violence of my birth. This was something each of us carried inside ourselves without understanding anything about its cause. My longing for her love never diminished.

Mothers Freed At Last

My mother was among the first generation of American women freed by baby formula from the necessity of breastfeeding. Just after the war, for the first time, infant formula became commercially available. Through aggressive advertising, and marketing by doctors and hospitals, bottle-feeding became a trend, the thing to do for upwardly mobile middle-class women.

Ma, like so many others, believed that formula was better than breast milk, that it was more nutritious! Plus you wouldn't be so tied down to your infant for constant feedings, and you wouldn't wreck your figure. (Nor would the sight of your boob in your baby's mouth discomfit your husband.) Never mind the many messes and inconveniences of bottle-feeding. Nobody ever mentioned those.

My mother, knowingly or not, was also among the legions of mid-century women who also gave up the contraceptive gift of breastfeeding (unreliable, yes, but an important factor in spacing children for generations of women around the world) in favor of commercial formula.

Ma did not breastfeed any of us. I didn't know that breastfeeding was humanly possible until I was 10 or 11, and one of my smart-ass cousins told me, a stunning revelation. Babies could suck milk from their mothers' boobies! *Who'd have thunk it?* Not me.

The kitchens of our many homes, the sinks and stoves, were always cluttered with the cans for powdered formula, glass bottles and screw-top rubber nipples in various stages of use and cleansing. The odiferous hand-mixed formula simmered in pots on the stove. (Equally odiferous cloth diapers languished in big buckets of ammonia in the bathroom.) We older girls, Jane and I, were often called upon to feed the babies. I'm certain I fed the youngest four as often as my mother did. I'd sit half comatose in front of a little black and white TV while Greg or Dan or Andrea or Amy sucked away at the bottle in my hand. Was I loving? Nurturing? I don't know! I loved my younger sisters and brothers, but what kid wants to be saddled with feeding an endless stream of hungry siblings?

I would not learn until decades later about the major role baby formula played in the epoch of closed newborn adoption.[3] The unholy trinity's focus on "rescuing" newborns from "bad" mothers was greatly enabled, perhaps accelerated, by the introduction in the early 1940s of commercial infant formula. Formula meant that women who'd just given birth were no longer required to remain in the mother and baby homes until their babies were weaned at two or even three years old. Instead, their babies could be taken away from them immediately after birth and fed with bottles. Intense marketing strategies by its producers continue to this day, including giving new mothers who plan to nurse, "gift packs" of formula in the hospital "just in case." A catastrophic shortage of infant formula in 2021 and 2022 (the result of global supply chain anomalies and changing regulations) revealed the vast and vital significance of manufactured infant formula.

As far back as I can remember, I was enlisted to feed and burb the babies, change their diapers and, when necessary, prop their bottles. Back then "propping" baby bottles was seen as an efficient alternative to the endless and boring task of holding an infant in yours arms for feeding.

In the 50s and 60s a trendy baby gift became a handmade "propping pillow," often done in eyelet, and embroidered, maybe with the baby's name, and a little blue or pink strap or envelope to hold the bottle in place near the baby's mouth. My mother, run ragged with all of her other household chores, used them often. We thought nothing of it. Prop a bottle near

---

3 As recounted in *Sticky Fingers,* Joe Hagan's biography of Jann Wenner, founder of Rolling Stone magazine, Wenner's California family earned its first fortune in the early 1940s by devising a way to safely manufacture and distribute baby formula.

a baby's mouth? Great idea! Feed the baby and go about your other household chores. Multitasking at its finest.

Lucky for new generations, research and advice by such pediatricians as Spock and Brazelton put an end to the widespread use of bottle proppers.

(Years later, in the 1990s, during the wild adoption booms from Romania and Russia, many orphaned adoptees were found to have incurable attachment disorders. No surprise to learn that most of their early nourishment came from propped bottles, now considered a particularly inhumane form of infant sustenance.)

For me, given my troubled history of motherhood, the act of breast-feeding helped erase my lingering doubts about my ability to mother my other (legitimate) children. I gloried in my ability to nourish on demand my other children, the first, a daughter Suzanne, born 15 years after Angus. It remains one of the pinnacle experiences of my life, intimacy and love in one of its purest forms. I'm thrilled that both of my daughters chose this most natural, and healthiest, practice with their babies.

Threatened

Today I make my slow way to the clinic for my regular prenatal checkup, a dreaded and always humiliating event. Never the same doctor. We rarely learn their names, and they do not say ours. Unless I ask a specific question, which I'm afraid to do, nobody bothers to tell me what's going on in my own body. I matter less than the baby my body holds.

In my seventh or eighth month, not long after my lunch date with my mother, fierce headaches began exploding inside my skull. Strange vision disturbances, bright zigzagging lines, warn of them. Except for their frequency and intensity, headaches are nothing new to me. I pay as little attention to them as possible. Anyway, my body, my big unwieldy body, no longer belonged to me but to the child it contained. Despite the tasteless food, I kept gaining weight. My hunger was never satisfied. My shoes didn't fit anymore. I felt him, yes, I was certain I was carrying a boy, rolling and stretching and hiccupping all hours of day and night. His presence was so clear, so dominant, that I shrank behind it.

I lumber into the nondescript examining room where a frilly-capped nurse takes my vitals. Her face tells me something's wrong. Yes, my blood pressure is off the charts and there's something wrong with my pee. I'm running a fever.

A resident comes in, one I've never seen before. He's heavy-set with deep brown eyes. Scrubs and a long white coat. He's serious. He focuses on me. He takes his time. He reads my chart, then takes hold first of my swollen left foot and then my right. He pokes them a couple of times with his index finger. Pink asterisks appear on the white skin. He checks my name and says it. Julia. Or do I prefer Julie? He repeats my vital signs, then say, 'Toxemia,' a word I have never heard before.

Then I'm on a gurney, being rushed upstairs to the hospital. Yes, upstairs I go, into one of the cell-like rooms reserved for girls from the home, girls too tainted by sin to be allowed any closer to the upscale private rooms where the real mothers are, the good mothers.

I was pinned to IVs and put on a diet of clear liquids; maybe medicated with unidentified substances. The next day or maybe the day after that, the resident came to check on me. 'Julie,' he called me and explained that I'd been suffering from preeclampsia, an ailment I'd also never heard of, basically another word for toxemia. A life-threatening condition, he said. *Life threatening.* The phrase rattled around in my brain, never to be forgotten.

I stayed in the hospital for a week with no access to TV or even radio. Jackie brought me some thick paperbacks, bestsellers that I ravened through. James Michener's *The Source* is the only one I remember. The resident came to see me one more time. He sat in a chair next to my bed and asked about my physical health and emotional health. At some point he asked, 'How did a girl like you end up here?' A girl like me? I was flattered, I couldn't help it, I warmed into his attention. I also understood that he'd accepted the cultural belief that unwed mothers were feckless sluts and he didn't think I fit into that category. He saw something about me that nobody else could see. I don't know what it was but it was a thrill: I was being recognized! But I couldn't answer his question. I couldn't tell him how I'd ended up there. I didn't understand myself. And now, as I write this, I bridle at his implied diss on the other girls, unrecognized at the time.

"Would you deliver my baby?" I asked him instead of answering. He smiled and said of course. If he were on call he would most definitely deliver my baby. I tucked this golden promise deep inside myself. I never saw him again.

My symptoms, extremely high blood pressure, protein in my urine, and sudden gain of water weight, were those of preeclampsia, signals of the deadly affliction eclampsia, also called toxemia. If left untreated, a pregnant woman will have seizures, go blind, and fall into a coma. Her baby, deprived of oxygen, will die in utero. It's a rare disorder these days in advanced countries due to careful prenatal screening, though it remains the major global cause of maternal death. It remains a particular hazard to first-time teen-age mothers and to women of color.

In May 2023, Tori Bowie, an Olympic track and field gold medalist in 2016, died along with her full term daughter when her preeclampsia evolved into eclampsia. Bowie, 32, lived alone and may well have lost consciousness before she knew what was going on, a tragic and unnecessary loss.

Eclampsia killed my maternal grandmother at 33, during the birth of her fifth daughter, my Aunt Josephine. It was Josephine herself who told me about the catastrophic childbirth complications of the mother she'd never known, Mary O'Degan Cushing. My missing grandmother. Dead at 33. My mother was six years old when this happened. But if she made any connection between her mother's death and my preeclampsia crisis, she never let on. We never spoke of it.

Bastards/Blue Ribbon Babies

Throughout history the offspring of unmarried women were labeled bastards, sons and daughters of whores, plain and simple. Even into the early years of the 20th century, out-of-wedlock babies were believed to be inferior, the damaged product of an illegal act or the result of a sinful union and, hence, essentially flawed. They deserved every bit of the scorn heaped upon them. Illegitimate children had no rights of inheritance no matter how wealthy their biological father happened to be.

Beginning in the early 1900s and lasting until the 40s, the American Eugenics Movement added fuel to the contempt heaped upon out-of-wedlock children. The eugenics movement held as its goal the elimination of undesirable human traits through selective breeding. It aimed to create a superior (white) race. Some 60,000 American women, mostly women of color, underwent forced sterilizations as the result of the Eugenics Movement. It was seen as a way to eliminate from humanity, once and for all, their "flawed" genetics. (More recently, from 1973 to 1976, according to the Government Accounting Office, almost 4,000 Native women were forcibly sterilized through Indian Health Service clinics, an important story line in the recent stellar AMC mystery series Dark Winds.)

Because of the prevailing revulsion over unmarried mothers and their children, adoption was rarely considered a solution to the growing problem of bastard babies. Throughout the 19th century and the early part of the 20th, nonfamily newborn adoption remained rare. Rather, mothers often stayed, and were often required to stay, in the mother-child homes for a year or two in order to breastfeed their babies until they could be weaned.

In Martin Sixsmith's bestselling history, *The Lost Child of Philomena Lee,* and the subsequent movie *Philomena,* starring Judi Dench, Philomena's son was three years old when he was snatched, without her knowledge or permission, from the Irish, nun-run mother and baby home where they'd been living together until that moment. This was a typical situation back then, the long period of breastfeeding, never mind the devastation for both mother and child when the child was taken.

Some shelters, notably the Booth homes, provided instructions on mothering and help finding resources that might enable the mothers to keep their children, as long as they were fully committed to being born again.

But as more and more out of wedlock kids were born in the 20s, 30s, and 40s, beliefs about the genetic inferiority of "illegitimate" babies began to crumble, according to the University of Oregon's Adoption Research Project. By then, unmarried mothers came not just from the poor and socially marginalized, but also from educated working class and middle-class families, mostly white. Their "good" bloodlines, a concept promoted by eugenics, couldn't be ignored. The changing class status of unwed mothers, cultural historians agree, eventually transformed "undesirable bastards" into unknowing innocents in need of rescue. Soon, they would come to be considered blue ribbon babies, like my son.

To answer more fully the question of how bastards turned into blue ribbon babies I followed the tangled vines of history back to the Southwest in the final years of the 18th century. In the decades following the Civil War and on into the pre – and post-World War I years, historians agree, it may have been a fate worse than death to be born a bastard or to be an orphaned or abandoned child. As a result of the war's devastations, this was a period of widespread abject poverty in both major cities and rural areas. Countless families had no income and lacked access to water or food or safe shelter. Such dire poverty motivated migrations from northern cities to the South and West, but no safety nets existed for children. Infants and children often died or were left to die along the trail. The concept of children as having inherent value, and needing special protections, was not yet clear.

During this period, orphaned and abandoned children lived short lives of intense suffering well outside any legal accountings. Only after they became visible, left to fend for themselves in the alleyways of major cities and along the trails of epic migrations, like today's homeless, were the consciences of the prosperous awakened. This was when, for the first and only time in American history, a large "domestic supply" of babies and children became available for adoption, if only someone would take them. (Note: catastrophe created this large "domestic supply" of children available for adoption, a phrase that made news in the 2022 in documents presented during the Supreme Court hearings before the demise of Roe V. Wade.)

The infamous Orphan Trains ran from the late 1800s until 1929, this nightmare period for the destitute children of America. It's believed that some 250,000 abandoned children were taken from orphanages and/or street corners in the East and sent out to rural areas in the Midwest and West on these trains. The children were basically given away to whatever families wanted them. Countless thousands were "adopted" into families only to serve as free labor on farms and businesses. Nobody kept count.

Not until 1912 was the first federal children's bureau created to help protect indigent children. Its first focus was preventing the exploitation of child labor. But more importantly, it marked the first time in our history that a government entity recognized the intrinsic worth of children whatever their ancestry.

In its early years, the federal government's creation of child welfare agencies failed to have much positive impact in the lives of vulnerable children. But it raised awareness about the obligations a society might have to them. Soon multiple state-funded child welfare agencies emerged. Some, unregulated and never monitored, were horrifically corrupt. Georgia Tann, for example, lives in infamy through books and movies. She ran the Tennessee Children's Home Society for about 40 years until her death in 1951. She is believed to have sold for profit at least 5,000 newborns whose births were never legally registered. She was never prosecuted.

The corruptions of some of the state-funded child welfare agencies notwithstanding, the great rebranding of American orphans and bastards was underway. Their transfiguration was the straw that the powerful eventually spun into the gold of the adoption fairy tale: people of good conscience, do-gooders, rescuing lost babies. Tucked inside this rescue impulse, like a fortune in a cookie, maybe read or maybe not, was the tacit belief that good married couples were entitled to children even if they could not produce them on their own.

In its 130-year history, the Gladney Center for Adoption exemplifies the changes in adoption practices based on changing perceptions of bastards and abandoned children. The Gladney Center is still considered by adoption advocates to be one of the most reputable agencies in the United States. On its website, it claims the "salvation of children" as its defining mission, one that has not changed in more than a century. (Working through Gladney, contemporary parents can expect to pay $52,000 for a domestic adoption, and between $40,000 and $50,000 for an international adoption. They're likely to wait years for either option. Its website promises ongoing support for birth mothers who relinquish and for adoptive parents after the child joins their family.)

Gladney traces its roots to the late 1880s, that grim period for parentless American children. That's when the domestic supply of orphaned and abandoned children exceeded the culture's ability to care for them. That's also when a circuit riding Methodist minister named I.Z.T. Morris, in his work along the Chisholm Trail, became alarmed by growing numbers of orphaned and abandoned children that he encountered in his work. In a widely heralded move, Morris publicly declared his intention of providing permanent homes and families for every one of them.

The Chisholm Trail, after the Civil War, was crucial to the economic rebuilding of the Southwest. Its history is inextricably linked with romances about the Wild West. Roughly 800 miles long, the legendary trail stretched from San Antonio, Texas to Abilene, Kansas. It was used to drive longhorn cattle overland from ranches in Texas to the railheads of Kansas, a three-month-long journey. Soon trains with cattle cars would make the trail obsolete, but not before Reverend Morris began his mission of finding or creating permanent safe housing for countless discarded children. To achieve it, Reverend Morris linked up, in the Fort Worth area, with the Texas Children's Home and Aid Society, an early state-funded child welfare agency managed by a young Edna Gladney. This connection between the minister and the social worker became an inflection point early in the history of American adoption.

Written histories confirm the many early arduous efforts of Morris and Gladney (among others in other locales) to find permanent homes and families for indigent children. Nobody has ever suggested that this wasn't good work. It was. However, over time, increasing American prosperity reduced the supply of parentless children available for adoption. By the late 1930s, the domestic supply had dwindled like a reservoir during drought. This created a dilemma for those who'd established themselves as adoption professionals, those whose reputations and livelihoods depended upon the creation and expansion of families via adoption. The ongoing, robust, and often reckless pre-marital activity of the young provided a solution, albeit an ironic one.

That's when the practice of separating bastard babies from their unmarried mothers first evolved, and along with it, the ever so alluring fairy tale of that plenary adoption, absolute and unconditional, was a win-win for everyone in the so-called triad, the baby, the first mother, and the adopting parents.

Gladney, personally and through her burgeoning agency, became one of the most successful marketers of closed infant adoption. By the years of the Baby Scoop, she also helped to navigate the shift in concern from truly orphaned and abandoned children to those not yet born to unmarried mothers.

This was a cataclysmic shift that very few historians have noticed or commented upon: the change from helping parentless children to taking children from unmarried parents and giving them to married couples. Gladney was just one among several who revolutionized American adoption practices in this way and helped to create the system of amended birth records and the court seal of the originals.

Gladney's proclamation, no illegitimate children, only illegitimate parents, still glows in an italic font on the Gladney website. Shocking though her words seem today, they were received as scripture by adoption professionals and have resonated in the adoption community ever since.

Gladney's expressed attitude justifies taking away the babies of unmarried women and giving them to more worthy parents. Neither its casual dismissal of unmarried mothers nor its cruelty toward biological parents was recognized. Rather, it flared into fact for the unholy trinity. No illegitimate babies, only illegitimate mothers and fathers.

By the middle of the past century, taking newborns from their unmarried mothers was standard operating procedure for a massive segment of the population: the white working and middle classes. By then it was deemed an enlightened solution to the massive and ever-growing public health problem of "promiscuous" girls and their bastard babies. Little thought was given to the fathers and none to the possible consequences for the mothers or their babies. The problem was the pathological sexuality of unmarried girls. It had to be gotten back under control. Its crude and cruel solution evolved into secret closed adoption.

Stirred into this cultural stew was the professionalization of social work. As confirmed in the work of Kunzel, Solinger, and the Adoption History Project, the wealthy volunteers who'd traditionally dealt with bad girls, fallen women, were gradually replaced in the 40s and 50s, by licensed social workers. The requirements for those early licensures are unclear. Moreover, research indicates, the first licensed social workers were mostly prosperous matrons who shared the same evangelical bent as their earlier unpaid sisters. Theirs was a missionary undertaking.

During those prosperous post-war years, children weren't merely a privilege of race and class for middle-class married couples. They were essential to participating in the America dream. In another facet of the religious and patriarchal vision of family, infertility in a married couple was deemed a shameful failure. The prosperous post-war Baby Boom (1946 to 1964) encompassed an unprecedented explosion of child-filled families. That's when another belief cultural conviction emerged: every middle-class white couple was entitled to children even if they could not produce them on their own. Not only were such good people entitled to babies, they were entitled to babies that looked just like them. That way nobody would ever question their fertility or shameful lack thereof. In the post-war years, "a chicken in every pot" morphed into "a child in every family." Children in the home were considered an essential aspect of the American Dream, as long as a married white couple headed the family. Hence, as the 20th century progressed, attention shifted away from rescuing bad mothers and turned toward rescuing instead their "at risk" children, never mind the mothers.

By the mid-40s onward, according to the University of Oregon's Adoption Research Project, illegitimacy was "reinterpreted as a sign of the mother's maladjustment and psychological disorder." Hence, secret adoption "appeared to be a positive solution." Adoption professionals who, just a few decades earlier "had worked so hard to keep natal families together … changed their mind about family preservation. Between 1940 and 1970 they acted upon the belief that placing children with married couples would save them from doomed lives with unmarried unstable mothers who could not offer them real love or security."

During these years, notions about the dangers posed by unmarried mothers simmered into a poisonous brew. Among its most potent ingredients were the convictions that an unwed mother and her child did not constitute a family and that the girl who relinquished her baby was healthier than the one who kept it.

Hard to imagine these days: That an unmarried mother and her baby are not a family! That an unmarried female who gives up her baby is healthier than the one who keeps it! In the second half of the 20th century, these ideas took hold in the adoption community with the bite force of a hyena. Hundreds of thousands of us felt the pain.

Following in Gladney's footsteps, in another part of the country, was another ardent advocate for closed newborn: Rose Bernstein, based at the Boston Crittenton home. Through her writing and public speaking, she, too, became a celebrity. Her ideas and Gladney's spread not unlike a toxic spill through the immediate pre – and post-war years, creating a playbook for caseworkers all over the country.

In her 1960 scholarly paper, "Are We Still Stereotyping Unmarried Mothers?" Bernstein accepts that the unmarried mother, no matter her age or familial situation, is pathological but she warns that each case deserved its own close analysis. "Our assumption that illegitimate pregnancy is invariably rooted in personality pathology has led us to accept uncritically certain further assumptions deriving from the basic one. That the same neurotic conflict which resulted in the out-of-wedlock pregnancy will motivate the girl in planning for her baby. Her decision about the baby is based not upon her feeling for him as a separate individual but upon the purpose for which she bore him."

In other words, the unmarried pregnant female had no actual understanding of what she was experiencing during her own pregnancy. She required professional help to realize relinquishment was the only possible path to getting her life back onto the right track!

Long before Bernstein's death, at 98, her writings had evolved into a strategic plan for social workers working with single mothers. These ideas were reinforced by her 1971 book *Helping Unmarried Mothers*. The headline of her Boston Globe obituary called her an "advocate for single parents."

It's safe now to say that the concepts Bernstein, Gladney and their colleagues, accepted and acted upon damaged, profoundly, the lives of so many young first mothers and their babies. I'm certain that my parents accepted them as fact when they banished me to the asylum in Dorchester. They were in play during my time at the "home." They still lurk in my life and also in the shadowy corners of Adoption Inc.

Best Interests

The doctrine of the "best interests of the child" soon blossomed among these tangled sociological and religious vines. It's a concept no one dares to dispute, but one that remains dangerously fluid for poor first mothers and women of color. In most states judges are required to decide what those 'best interests' are in court adjudications regarding minor children, whether or not they have an interest in child welfare or any skill in deploying it. Babies and children are often taken from addicted mothers or mothers with mental health issues, but rarely are these mothers provided with the help they need to keep their children.

Back in the day, "best interests" required that the label "bastard" never be attached to out-of-wedlock children. Hence, the slut mother had to be "encouraged" to give away her baby as soon as possible after birth. That way the baby could go out into the world unstained by illegitimacy, with the new birth certificate that erased his or her shameful conception.

This philosophy was in full flower when my parents left me off at St. Mary's. Even though I did not know it, it's what overwhelmed me during my pregnancy, my time at the home, and the loss of my child. I was illegitimate. I was pathological. I have never fully recovered.

PART FOUR

Home Stretch

M any memories of my time at home have gone blurry, like a tap-
estry, perhaps valuable at one time but shabby now, musty, faded
by inappropriate storage, and its delicate stitching, once brought
out into the light, vulnerable to disintegration. Hard to imagine now, let
alone remember, that as many as one hundred of us at a time wandered
those shadowy corridors together, every one of us banished from our
families, our baby daddies nowhere to be found. We wandered there
in our bedraggled maternity smocks and whatever footwear we could
squeeze onto our feet.

My entire time at St. Mary's Infant Asylum I was surrounded by
other pregnant girls. We ate together, cleaned together, prayed together,
played cards and Monopoly together but rarely shared any intimate
details about our lives. We enjoyed gossiping about the nuns and com-
plaining about the food and our clinic check-ups but we skirted around
talk about how we got pregnant or our future plans. Our daily life was
geared toward prayer and silence, and the refusal to acknowledge or
to share our sense of what was really going on: that we were serving as
breeders for infertile couples. We did not become friends.

One girl, however, remained passionately in love with the father of
her baby bragged about the special nature of their love. She detailed their
plans to defy her parents, to elope and to have another baby as soon as
she turned 18. After their first child was adopted, of course. I envied her,
both her love and her dreams.

Despite our best efforts to find out how we'd ended up where we'd
ended up, we remained ignorant, every one of us, about what the future
held, the suffering we'd face, in both the immediate and the distant future.
The girls who left to give birth at St. Margaret's across the way were not

allowed to return. The doors to the hospital only went one way. When a girl in labor left for the hospital, we would not see her again. No chance, that way, that the new mothers could tell us their stories. They couldn't tell us what labor felt like or what it felt like when their baby disappeared.

The terrible year of 1966 is coming to a close, New Year's Eve, and my time is also drawing near. I'm so filled with child that I have trouble sleeping, trouble getting comfortable. Tonight, after lights out, a half a dozen of us, or maybe more, sneak into a common room. We made our plan surreptitiously, during lunch or supper, whispering behind our hands. Somebody has a radio, a small transistor radio no doubt sneaked into the home and hidden by its owner. (Such entertainments aren't allowed.) We gather quietly, leaning in toward that little radio with its tinny sound. We're searching for our music, we outcasts with our big bellies, on the verge of delivering babies that will be snatched from us.

We girls, mostly teen-agers, gather around it hoping for a clear Top 40 station. We want the big hits from *Herman's Hermits, Lovin' Spoonful, Mamas and Papas, Dave Clark Five,* music from the world we used to live in. Among the favorites blaring from that tiny radio, are Devil in a Blue Dress, Mustang Sally and the *Beach Boys'* Good Vibrations. *Good fucking vibrations. Excitations! Hahaha.* Tunes and lyrics we already know by heart. We sing along but softly so as not to wake the nuns.

In socks and slippers, or maybe barefoot, and maternity nighties fashioned by Omar the Tentmaker, we dance and prance, and spin and leap. We twist and frug and hitchhike, teaching each other our best moves. We do the shimmy, the mashed potato, and the locomotion. I crank out a few splits, Chuck Berry style. We do jumping jacks and other calisthenics forbidden to those in our condition. On purpose. We're hoping to jump start labor. Time and again, we collapse in laughter. We can't stop. Our confinement and humiliation waft out into the winter night as we reclaim our right to dance, to laugh, to be teenagers. Eventually, exhausted, we tiptoe back to our rooms, our little beds, to begin the New Year, 1967. (Not until I was in the midst of writing this story did I realize this happened exactly one year after I lost my virginity.)

Delivery Day

Back when Daddy drove me to St. Mary's in our family's new white station wagon (my baby bump just visible, my baby already swimming inside me) I couldn't foresee that the experience of birthing and losing a child would change me forever. I could not grasp that. Even so, I figured I'd be alone through everything that happened at the "asylum" and in the aftermath of my stay. I was right about the aloneness but ignorant about what it would mean. In the weeks and months ahead I'd find out. I'd learn what true loneliness meant, a place I've been back to more than once in my long life. But back then I didn't, and couldn't, imagine what awaited me.

I don't remember when my contractions began, those strange ripples deep inside my body, so deep and so strange, not yet excruciating, but most definitely heralding the birth. Some time on January 2, soon after our communal New Years Eve foray into fun and laughter. I remember but only vaguely, my hasty good-byes to the other girls, their excitement that another one of us was "getting out." I'd never see any of them again.

All of us knew our contractions had to be regular and well under way before we got taken, accompanied on foot or in a wheelchair, depending, to the hospital via a series of corridors and staircases. Were there tunnels? Subterranean hallways? I cannot say for sure but that is what it felt like to me. After all, we were the hidden girls. No one in the outside world could see us, our shame, and we could not see them. I have no memory of going over to the hospital, of who brought me over and got me admitted.

A so-called labor room was hidden from the rest of the floor where the real mothers were. Windowless. A big dark closet with a bed in the middle and me on the bed. Alone in the small room, terror closing in. Soon, nurses in white uniforms and frilly caps show up to shave off my pubic hair and give me an enema. SOP. They do not speak to me. I guess I'm unspeakable.

They strap me to the bed (did this really happen? Or did it only feel like it?) so I cannot get away or hurt myself trying to escape the thundering pain. (I've kept that inside me ever since.) No epidurals, no other analgesics that I recall. I had to suffer. We were meant to suffer, the cost of our redemption. Expiation. Absolution. Although once during that long night a nurse came in and shoved a wet face cloth, wrung into a hard cylinder, into my mouth. *You're making too much noise,* she said. *Bite down when the pain is bad.*

I have no idea how long I was in labor, maybe eight hours, maybe 12. No records were kept of such things. (My son's original birth certificate states that he was born at 9:45 pm on a Tuesday, January 3.) But, at long last the crowning and a quick skid into the delivery room. By then I was dizzy, mindless with pain, understanding only vaguely what's going on. A young resident I'd never seen before, not the kind one I'd been hoping for, rushes into the delivery room. Preppy in his white coat and horn-rimmed glasses. "Want me to adjust that mirror so you can watch the birth?" he asked, pointing to the one over the delivery table. A nurse jabbed him. "She's a girl from the home," she whispered, loud enough for me to hear. He turned the mirror away. He didn't look at me or speak to me again. A beast on the table, a breeder. This flashbulb moment scorched into my mind. I've never been able to get it back out.

A quick episiotomy and then the birth, a big screaming baby boy. A blue-ribbon baby! Everyone understands this description, most especially the woman, me, who has just pushed him, wailing, into the world. But the words are only whispered, never said out loud. Blue-ribbon baby. Healthy. White. A prize for the family he would go to, a family far more prosperous, more able, than this unmarried teen-ager bleeding on the table. More worthy. Nature may have denied them the ability to reproduce one on their own but they are, everyone with power agrees, entitled to him.

I heard him before I saw him, red and slimy, flailing into the world. I reached for him. The nuns or maybe the nurses, or maybe the nuns were nurses, held me back. More than anything I wanted to hold onto my baby boy, to keep him close, this son I'd been carrying inside, so heavily and sorrowfully and lovingly, all this time. Yes, I loved my baby, would forever, the baby with whom I'd been cast into exile. I wanted to get my hands on him. My hands needed to touch him, my heart too. My mouth. I had to nuzzle him and kiss him. If I could only hold him and keep him close, then everything in my world would be OK. Possible. But no. They take him away. I catch a glimpse just before he disappears, a big ferocious boy who will belong to someone else. The ghost baby born away.

No, no, they kept telling me as they worked me over, and I fought them, bloodied and exhausted. They injected my breasts with hormones to dry up my milk. Ergotrate for my uterus. Something to make me sleep. Another great commotion followed, entwined with more whispered words: *Contamination! Disinfection!* Nobody told me anything. I didn't exist for them. Women, maybe nuns or nurses, rushed around to drape the delivery room in sterile white sheets: the space will require special disinfection before the next laboring mother will be allowed in. I, the locus of filth, was wheeled out of it. *The not mother. Hide her.* I woke up in another room, emptied and anguished, no baby, and plenty of time to think about the mess I'd made out of my life.

Broken Promise

My isolated room was nearly, but not quite, hidden from the rest of the maternity floor. Day and night for two endless days I listened to the cacophony of crying newborns, and to the joyful comings and goings of the new moms and dads. Card, flowers, many visitors! But I did not have my baby. He was in the nursery, in a bassinette, with a handwritten note attached: Baby Boy MacDonnell. I could walk down the hallway to see him through the window of the nursery. He was parked there with all the other babies, the legitimate ones. You couldn't tell the difference by looking at him. But I was not allowed to touch him. They refused to bring him to me and refused to tell me why. Every time I went to the nursery window, I was firmly escorted back to my room. I don't know who 'they' were. I don't remember who did the escorting.

For two days, hormones and pain and unknown medications swirled inside me as I edged toward a psychotic break. I fought to hold my baby. I asked nurse after nurse, unable to accept this betrayal of Jackie's and my caseworker's promise. They ignored me. I don't remember a doctor ever coming to check on me, but one must have and I must have asked him, too.

Toward the end of the second day I had a breakdown, or that, at least, is what Jackie told me afterward. I have only the blurriest recollection of pounding on the nursery windows, gazing through them, as if through drenching rain, wailing for my sleeping son. Jackie confirmed that I shrieked and hollered in the hallway outside the nursery. "You upset everyone," she said. (Another example of my pathology.) She said she thought I was more mature than that. She said they (who?) sedated me and hauled me back to my bed, an embarrassing scene, so distressing for all those other new moms and dads.

The next morning, however, Jackie reappeared in my doorway. "The nurses will bring him in for the next feeding," she said. "Just to be on the safe side." Safe side? To prevent me from succumbing to permanent madness? To prevent me from bothering the other new mothers on the floor? She said she told them (who?) it would be best for me to see and hold my baby before he was gone for good. She didn't say anything about the promise; or why he'd been kept from me. I did not have the presence of mind to ask. Fifty years would pass before I learned the answer. I've never stopped mourning those two lost days with my son.

Surrender

E arly in the morning, the nurses wheel the newborns from the nursery into their mothers' rooms for the first feeding of the day. It's a ritual, this parading of the newborns in shiny bassinettes down the gleaming hallways of this prestigious hospital for women. St. Margaret's Lying in Hospital. Lying in: a place of rest after giving birth, a privilege available to well-insured urban and suburban wives. The baby parade creates a soft rumble in the hallways that all the new mothers anticipate.

I, too, am a new mother. I, too, hear the parade heralding the arrival of the babies. But I am not one of them: no ring on my finger, no loving husband waiting to take me home. I am one of the hidden ones, the wanton girls who, for a price, have been sequestered in the Georgian mansion next door, St. Mary's Infant Asylum, to await the births of our misbegotten children.

No cards or flowers or balloons in the room where I wait. Just me, sitting on the bed in street clothes, a baggy shirt, maybe even a maternity smock, big enough to cover my still swollen belly. I just turned 19, a birthday nobody, not even me, celebrated. Because I am worse than a disgrace, a blight upon the shiny fabric of my family and the culture: an unwed teenage mother.

A not mother.

For the past 48 or 54 or 60 hours, since my son's birth, endless hours, I've sat here on the bed in this stark room listening to the joyful cries and chatter of husbands and wives and newborns celebrating the beginning of their lives together, the oohs and ahhs of their visitors. I have heard them but not seen them. My room is down a dimmer corridor, tucked away from the others. In my mind's eye, I see the nurse who is approaching: she wears a starched white dress, white stockings and white oxfords. A frilly cap is perched proudly on her head.

She is bringing me my son, but she will not look at me or speak to me. She does not approve of me and makes sure I know this. Like the other nurses and nuns and doctors and social workers and counselors who poke me and prod me, berate me and humiliate me, she believes I should be banned from seeing or feeding my own baby. That is the best way. That is what they all believe, and what happens most of the time. It's a hot conviction, a lozenge on which she and all the others suck: I don't deserve to see or hold my baby. But she does what she's been told to do – she brings my baby to me. She leaves him in his bassinet just inside the door. I rush to him. He is rosy and robust, my baby, just a few days old.

I have named him Angus after my loved grandfather, though my grandfather will never learn of his existence, this namesake, his first great-grandchild. I savor his baby smell, the softness of his skin. I can hardly believe his perfection, the wonder of his being, his strength and beauty after all those anguished and agonized months of pregnancy, of carrying him, of shame hurled at me from every corner, and me shrinking from shame, about to disappear.

I kiss the soles of his feet, his tiny fingers. I take my time.

Here, holding Angus, I am inside a soft impenetrable fog. This fog protects me from sorrow and confusion and physical pain and exhaustion, everything I have been through these past few days, and what I know is coming next.

Here, in the fog, I understand that I slipped out of my own body when the baby slipped out of mine. The anguish in my heart, my body, unacknowledged by anyone around me, was more than I could bear. I slipped away. I began to watch, as if from a great distance, all that was happening.

Today I'm going home. I'm going home with my mother and father but not my son. I will be going to the home I share with five sisters and two brothers, and the parents who have reviled me, who have abandoned me and also their first grandchild. I will be going home, a place of chronic conflict that often slides into humiliation and violence. My future will not formulate. It is a dark blur.

Angus is here now. I take him, and the bottle of formula from the bassinet. I hold him close to feed him. (Among the many mysterious procedures I have endured, my breasts have been injected with a chemical, diethylstilbestrol, to dry up my milk. Nobody asked me. Nobody explained.)

Just me and my baby in our cloud, a place of warmth and light. He slurps contentedly. I have loved him from the moment I first felt him move. Now my love pours out of me, sweet and warm as milk. I watch and listen, feeling how he needs me, needs this nourishment. I imprint the sights and sounds of his hunger, his sweetness, so that I can carry them inside myself forever. The milk in the glass bottle disappears too fast, too fast. I hold him a few more minutes even while he sucks on the empty bottle. After that, I strip him and wash him all over with a warm wet facecloth. Again I kiss his belly, his fingers, and his toes. I want my touch, my love, to imprint.

I put on a fresh diaper, a cloth one with big safety pins, a skill I learned long ago caring for my sisters and brothers. I dress him in footie PJs, a hat and little mittens. I wrap him in a matching bunting to keep him warm on the next part of his journey. His clothing is white with red trimming, part of a layette my mother, directed by the caseworker, bought for him before his birth, before anyone knew his gender. After we get home, she will hand me a crumpled receipt for the layette, and demand to be repaid.)

I dress Angus carefully, the final task I will perform as his mother. In minutes, when I'm finished, my social worker will take him. No turning back. And my parents will take me home. That was the deal, written in my own blood: give up the baby and you may come home. Otherwise, you're on your own.

Too Soon

At last, the moment arrives; the moment I knew would happen without knowing how to get ready for it. I carry Angus out into the foyer by an elevator. My parents and my caseworker wait. I have no feelings, all lost somewhere inside or outside myself. Only in retrospect did I see the scene: the caseworker, a skinny self-certain spinster employed by Catholic Charities of Greater Boston, a woman with all the answers. She's been giving them to my parents for months, since the previous summer when I couldn't hide my condition anymore. I think Ma and Daddy love her more than they love me. They believe everything she tells them.

They have been waiting for this moment, Ma and Daddy, longing for it, the turning point, when they will at last be relieved of the terrible burden of my sins, my trespasses, my willful defiance of their rules, my errors in judgment, my bad choices.

They've been waiting since August, waiting, waiting, waiting, for the moment when my baby will be whisked away as if he'd never existed, and they won't yet become grandparents. The relief: life at home will go back to normal. They will put all of this behind them, the chaos and shame created by me, their good-for-nothing daughter. Nobody else will ever have to know what a slut she is. For them, this experience will disappear like a stone tossed into a lake. It will make a small splash and then disappear.

With a rueful smile, a smile!, my caseworker takes Angus from my arms. He's awake, looking all around with his alert big eyes, but he does not cry. Angus, his warmth, his heft, his silky skin.

"You'll forget all about him," she promises for the umpteenth time as she heads for the elevator. "You'll go on with your life as if this never happened." Then she and my baby are gone.

PART FIVE

Silence Is A Plan

My parents' silence on the drive back home from St. Mary's Infant Asylum became their *modus vivendi* for dealing with me, their wretched daughter. It remained in force for the rest of their lives, and our lives together: What had happened had not happened.

Except in regard to that one legal loose end, the termination of my parental rights to my baby, neither parent ever again spoke of my experience. Neither one ever again acknowledged the existence of my son, their first grandchild. Not one word. Not ever. No forgiveness. No reconciliation or reconnection. No dying declarations from either of them. Silence.

Back home, in silence, I hid myself away. I hid every real and important thing about myself. I became a palimpsest of myself, a shadow of the person I'd started out to be. Instead of the busy, life-loving girl I'd been, the aspiring dancer and/or poet, I turned mute and sullen. No more dancing. That had been another me. The new one was emptied out, deflated, unable to move. I was afraid to cry because if I started, I wouldn't be able to stop. And, anyway, I did not have a private place to cry. Six of us kids shared one bathroom, our bedrooms crammed into the walkout basement of the house. Somebody was always banging on the bathroom door, which did not have a lock, and yelling, "Hurry up." I could not show any feeling to my parents or to my brothers and sisters, and I didn't.

A few weeks later I was matriculated as a second semester freshman at a small Catholic college just south of Boston where Jane could keep an eye on me. We'd commute together. Daddy had arranged this. He was giving me, he said, a second chance.

Bad Dreams

In my journals from that period after I left the asylum and again became a fulltime student, I find notes about recurrent dreams of catastrophic loss. In my journals, I leaned toward poetry, recounting my dreams of girls who had lost everything, girls who lost themselves. Not once do I mention the loss of my son. The secret is buried so deep that I cannot access it even in my most private journals. Instead, I dreamed of girls being stripped and starved and beaten; of girls trying to escape; girls scrambling over trash heaps, slag heaps, oil-slicked edges of polluted seas, girls who, even as they scrambled, kept hunting for something of value. Sometimes the lost girl was me; other times, my mother or the maternal grandmother I never knew. Often, in the dreams, as noted in my journals, I heard the sound of a door opening and closing, opening and closing, but I couldn't find the door. I'd search and search, following the sound, but I never found it. Now and then, the girl in the dream held a doorknob. Sometimes the doorknob was brass, tarnished and dented. Sometimes it was made of glass, shimmering like an enormous gem, a precious or semi-precious mineral pressed from generations of sorrow. In my dreams I conflated the girl and her mother, blurred their boundaries, bound them together, flesh of one another's flesh; spirit of one another's spirit; our intimacy profound, eternal, not anything at all like the one my mother and I really shared.

Acquiescense

After I relinquished my child, I acquiesced to the familial and cultural narrative that I was a quasi-criminal, a boundary-breaker who deserved severe punishment. I was a girl who went away, an unwed teenage mother who'd earned every moment of her misery. Ever after I had to watch my step. I never stopped trying to become the "good girl" my parents wanted me to be. I could not yet admit to myself how badly my parents had mistreated me. I knew that everything was my own fault.

I married young, and quickly, to a smart and loyal man who happened to be Chinese. He was a solitary immigrant from the Fiji Islands, an orphan with a biography even more complex and loss-laden than my own. His closest relatives lived many thousands of miles away. (We met in the wake of the May 4, 1970, murders of four Kent State University student protesters and the wounding of nine others by the Ohio National Guard, an event that shut down campuses all across the United States, including our own, Stonehill, in North Easton, Massachusetts.) We created lives for ourselves and we created our own family. We were married for 35 years.

Starting out, it was just the two of us and we made a life together. We did this without financial or emotional support from anyone. It was the two of us against the world. After college, we moved first to the Lower East Side of Manhattan and then, as urban homesteaders, to the Bronx where we rehabbed a 10-unit apartment building with our friends, mostly community organizers and veterans of the anti-war movement. Eventually, we, the group of us, purchased the building for $2500 from the city and turned it into a tenant owned coop, 2674 Valentine Avenue. It is still going strong. We lived there for seven years, among the happiest of my life. (Others in our group remain my chosen family, my dearest lifelong friends.) I doubt our frugal and adventurous path is available to young people any longer.

My husband and I shared quirky senses of humor, progressive politics, a love of music and exotic food. We were an interracial couple long before it became common and we positioned ourselves on the margins of the culture as witnesses and critics.

I went on to earn two graduate degrees. In the early 1980s, as the result of my husband's work, we left New York City and bought a home in southern New Jersey, just outside Philadelphia. We had three children. (In 1990 we adopted the youngest, our cherished daughter Marisa, from Peru, a nation at that time torn apart by the Shining Path guerilla war.) Throughout my kids' growing years, I competed to be the best mother ever: room mother, school trip chaperone, teacher of crafts to kids, cutter of oranges for sports events. Also, the tireless hostess of sleepovers, pumpkin cutting parties and Easter egg hunts, the chauffeur of events too numerous and far-flung to declare. I loved every minute.

Yes, I loved being a mother but I also had a career. I still longed to "make something" of myself even though I also had to support my family. I published short stories in prestigious little magazines and then a novel with major house. I won some grants and fellowships for my literary writing. I earned tenure at a public university, served as the nonfiction editor of Philadelphia Stories, a literary quarterly. I accomplished all of these things with the steadfast support of my husband. Nevertheless I remained obsessed with earning my parents' devotion along with intimacy and respect from my siblings. I fawned. I begged for love. I did everything I could to ensure it. Even so I always felt precarious, unworthy, as if, at any moment, I could lose everything. I knew that I could lose everything. It had happened once before.

Searching Back Then

I n 1984, I was pregnant with my third child, my second legitimate child, (my loved son Gabriel), when I decided the time had come for me to search for Angus. Finding Angus, reuniting with him, in a warm and glorious moment of reconciliation, had been in my heart since the day my caseworker walked off with him. This fantasy was attached like a barnacle in the dark space of my subconscious where it developed an impenetrable crust, and required no sustenance to keep it there.

Angus would turn 18 on January 3, 1985. Being of legal age, I figured he'd be free to make his own decisions about his origins. He'd be free to find his genetic history. And I just knew that Angus would want to find me as much as I wanted to find him.

But closed adoption leaves no paper trail. Like the vast majority of birth mothers, I had nothing to go on when I decided to search. No copy of his birth certificate, neither the original, nor the "amended" one that would reveal his new name, and the names of his new parents. No copy of the "voluntary termination of parental rights" that I would have had to sign for the adoption to move forward. Nothing. I didn't even remember the name of the asylum or hospital, a not uncommon phenomenon among us birth mothers. I'd surrounded myself in a dense fog, keeping, as I'd been advised to, the dangerous secret of my past. I kept the hidden girl hidden.

The birth of our daughter Suzanne in 1982 opened a glorious new chapter in my life. I loved being a mother and I couldn't wait to have another child. But then I also, as often happens with first mothers, felt more deeply the loss of my first son. To ease that pain, I convinced myself that my lost son and I would easily find each other. I believed, head still in the clouds, that ever so pleasing dream world, that he'd become integrated into my young family – not by any means abandoning his adoptive family – but adding a new one, a blended family. (I could not imagine any tumult or conflict in such a reunion. My imagination deemed it not entirely possible, but even probable.)

But then I got Catholic Charities' letter declaring that they had no record of my son's adoption, or of me. I was mystified and enraged, but also helpless. I knew I'd given up a baby, and I knew Catholic Charities had done the deal. Again, that terrible feeling of having been discarded, and only incidental to the adoption of my son flooded in my mind and heart. (I could have asked my father for those details but I didn't. Could have but couldn't and didn't. I assented to silence in order to remain his daughter, part of his family. I never asked him anything. I was afraid to and my chronic low-grade fear sometimes blossomed into panic.)

Works Of Mercy

During my time at the unwed mothers home I had passed holidays and some weekends at the home of a nearby family. I became friends, or I thought I was a friend, with the wife and mother of this family. I'll call her Hannah. She was, when I knew her, a 30-something mother of four young children, an ardent Catholic, who volunteered to help girls at the home through their time there. For the devout, such volunteer work would be considered a corporal and spiritual "work of mercy," helping to pave the way to heaven.

By coincidence she lived in the same pricey Boston suburb where my father eventually made his last stop. One day, while at his home in the early 1980s, I looked her up in the phone book and there she was. She could supply some important puzzle pieces. I called her. She remembered me and we chatted pleasantly for a couple of minutes. After that, I wrote to her.

'The intense agony of his loss has never left me, not for a moment in 18 years. The birth of Suzanne and the imminent birth of my third child – joyful, precious events – have made only more compelling my desire to find my first-born. I must know who he is and that he is all right. I am certain with every fiber of my being that he wants this information as much as I want to give it to him. I am determined to pursue my search. I think it is the only way I can be completely healed. '

Rereading my letter after of many years, I note my theatrical eloquence. I was trying to impress Hannah. I was determined for her to understand that I was no longer a borderline delinquent, a college flunkout, and a slut. I'd completed my education! I had a graduate degree from an Ivy League university. I was a married parent! We owned a home! I closed my letter with this question: *What are your thoughts on this?* I waited forever for her response. In her brief return letter, just a note, really, Hannah advised, *"Leave well enough alone."*

I was crushed. Well enough? *Well enough!* By whose measure? Not mine!

But, in her note, she included a copy of a recent newsletter for Catholic Family Services for the Diocese of Greater Boston. It turned out to be more valuable than her support: the name of the asylum where I'd been confined, the name of my caseworker and the particular Catholic Charities office through which the adoption was arranged, in Lynn, Massachusetts. It was, in fact, part of the Boston office, but I would eventually learn that they'd moved since the adoption and had misplaced my records during the move. Decades passed before they found them.

I called the Lynn office. Before they could tell me anything, including that the adoption had occurred, that I had to send a certified, notarized letter, along with a check for $25, requesting "non-identifying information."

I gathered those items and included an additional statement for his file: that I was willing to be contacted if my surrendered son ever wanted to find me. I took these items to a notary at our bank downtown on the White Horse Pike, scalded with humiliation as he glanced through the contents. Then I sent them off.

Weeks later, I received, from Catholic Charities the summary of a social worker's visit to my son's new home (no address included) dated in 1969. It described him, at 18 months old, as a robust blue-eyed boy, crawling and half walking, and full of energy. He was good-natured and prone to nasal congestion. That was it!

Yet I was relieved by the reality, there, in writing, on a piece of paper, that my son actually existed. This was the first documentary confirmation of his existence, eighteen years after the fact. I wasn't crazy, after all, the way I sometimes felt, because no one in my life had ever acknowledged his existence.

By law, Catholic Charities couldn't share any record of my son's birth adoption without his permission. But my son couldn't give his permission because he didn't have a legal right to see his own original birth record. Unless his adoptive parents had told him, which they had no legal obligation to do, he wouldn't even know that he was adopted or where information about it might be found. He would have no way to know that I'd asked.

Back then, before the advent of Internet technology, I registered with the International Soundex Registry, a free mutual consent registry, founded in 1975 by open-records advocate Florence Fisher. Their purposes was, is, to reunite anyone who has been separated from a family member due to adoption, divorce, or foster care. Until the early 2000s, and the emergence of commerical DNA databases, this registry and similar more costly ones, were the only way, other than using private investigators, that family members could signal that they were searching and hoping for reconnection. Even so I doubted that my teenage son would have had the wherewithal to register himself.

I understood that Catholic Charities held all the cards and they were, like all the big agencies, determined to keep those cards close, and keep their closed records closed. That was the end of my search. My son Gabriel was born a couple of months later and I was swept into another wave of maternal jubilation. I tamped down my rage and helplessness, not knowing that they lingered in that hidden place inside me.

Through all those years and decades, it nagged me that I had never seen the signed surrender of my parental rights! I did not remember signing it, no matter how hard I tried. Of course, I had no legal right to see it, but as time went on, I began to wonder if my signature had been forged. By then, in the mid-80s, I was living deeply in the beautiful ecology of young motherhood. I was the mother of a daughter I loved beyond measure and was pregnant with a son whose birth is among the greatest moments of my life. I felt so lucky and so blessed. In that mindset, I doubted that I would ever have been capable of signing away my parental rights to a baby. Especially in a place like Massachusetts where there is no grace period. Which means a parent cannot change their mind once their signature is on the document. Not even five or ten minutes later. The moment the parent (almost always the birth mother) signs, their parental rights are forever severed, and their baby is gone for good.

No, I decided, I could not have signed such a document. I began to wonder if my son's adoption had been legal. I began to imagine that someone else signed the termination of my parental rights. Even in my fog, I knew the players of the unholy trinity were capable of anything.

Remedies

During my decades of raising children, I went through many years of therapy, examining and trying to correct my many flaws, to find the cause of my seemingly inexplicable suffering. As I saw it, everything was my own fault. None of my therapists ever fully disagreed. I guess I was an emotional outlier, as self-protective as a rock face, even though I didn't know it. I was prescribed many medications, some of which helped and some that did not.

The therapists focused mainly on what they called my dysthymia, my adjustment disorder: an inability to properly calibrate to the circumstances of my own life. Only once, just once in all those years, not long after my failed search, did I discuss my early motherhood and loss. The therapist considered it irrelevant. Let's deal with what's happening in your life now, she said. Treat the loss of the baby like a death. Move on. After that, my vow of silence extended to those 50-minute hours with skilled professionals trying to help me to feel better about myself without understanding what the actual problem was. I didn't know myself. Only after my surrendered son found me did I begin to understand.

For most of my adult life I lived in the fog, the most comfortable place to be. A gentle mist surrounded me, obscuring certain realities and protecting me as I went on with my life. Domestic adoption matters were of little concern to me. I ignored them. I was determined to remain a member of my own family and determined to be loved by them. I'd be a great mother to my other children while pretending that I did not suffer from what had happened to me so long ago. Still, I half believed the things those powerful grown-ups had said about me back when my sense of self was as permeable as a veil, about my unworthiness, my failings. I never had the wherewithal to fight back, to explain myself to my family or to anyone else. Silent ignorance was my ticket.

I had no idea that, by the 1970s, an adoption reform movement, driven mostly by adult adoptees, had rooted in the United States. This movement hoped to reveal the special difficulties of adoptive kinship and assert the need for adoptees to learn their genetic identities, which the United Nations considers a basic human right. As recounted in her 1973 memoir, "The Search for Anna Fisher," the first adoption search memoir, Fisher searched for decades to find her first parents, raging over amended birth certificates and closed records. In addition to developing the International Soundex Registry, Fisher founded the Adoption Liberty Movement Association (ALMA) with a national reach and tens of thousands of members.

A few years after ALMA was created, Lee Campbell, a birth mother in Boston, founded Concerned United Birth Parents (CUB) the organization that, for the first time in known history, shined an empathetic light on the experiences of those who'd given up children to adoption, voluntarily or otherwise. Back then, both Fisher and Campbell used classified newspaper ads to find others like themselves. Both were, reportedly, overwhelmed by the responses they received.

By the mid-1990s, unknown to me, a network of groups like ALMA, CUB, and Bastard Nation were digging away at the foundations of the win-win adoption fairy tale. They advocated vociferously and cogently for open adoption records, and against family separation. They argued that adoptees, all the many millions of them, had a basic right to know their biological identities and the details of their births and surrender.

In my fog, I had no idea of the shattering impact, beginning in the early 2000s, that commercial databases would have on the secrets of adoption and biological parentage. Two never-before-heard-of categories have emerged among those most impacted by adoption: what are now labeled NPEs, or Not Parent Expected, and LDAs, for Late Discovery Adoptees. As yet uncounted thousands of them. These new categories have expanded the traditional 'adoption triad' into the preferred 'adoption constellation.' (Both best-selling author Dani Shapiro, and actor Kerry Washington are among the newly recognized NPEs though neither was adopted. They have written memoirs that movingly tell how they discovered, through DNA testing, that the loved fathers who raised them were not their biological fathers.)

Massachusetts, where I gave birth, was in the vanguard with regard to opening its sealed adoption records. It first did so, for certain groups of adult adoptees in 2008, thus, eventually, enabling my son, to find me.

Golden Fairy Tale

By the late 30s and early 40s, a divine myth had developed around the practice of closed infant adoption. This evolved soon after growing American prosperity had reduced drastically that vast 'domestic supply' of adoptable infants and children so crucial to the Adoption Industrial Complex. Hardly anyone noticed or cared that it was a fairy tale, written entirely to the benefit of its authors. It was a dazzling success.

The foremost plot point: that closed newborn adoption was a win-win for everyone involved. Not only that, but taking newborns from their mothers, the sooner the better, created families that were identical to biological families, thus alleviating the anguish of infertility for countless married couples. Not to mention that this practice was an excellent solution to the explosion bastard babies that had been polluting the population of pre – and post-war America. All those young people (no access to reliable contraception) screwing around, ignoring the sexual mores of their parents! The dominant image of this myth was the beautiful white baby, rescued from mysterious threats, nestled all snug and safe in the arms of its loving new parents. The new parents, this heart-warming image suggests, were perfect. They're prosperous and they own a home somewhere safe, where the child will grow up in happy innocence.

It says nary a word about how or why the baby became available for adoption. It also fails to note the erasure of the "rescued" baby's name and history, its mother's childbirth experience. The baby is, in fact, a changeling, like in a fairy tale, though no one in the Adoption Industrial Complex ever calls them that.

In the win-win adoption myth, other elements of fairy tale abound either explicitly or implicitly: the clash between good (adopting parents, caseworkers, counselors and many varieties of religious) and evil (the wanton child-bearers, the illegitimate parents); the rescue of innocent babies followed by the babies' magical transformation into a new identity they'd know nothing about. In this beguiling tale, the couples that open their hearts and wallets to welcome the babies of other mothers into their families, are deemed saviors. They are, after all, rescuing unwanted and discarded bastards from lives of shame. "Happily ever after" is the enduring promise of this story. No kinship or identity issues ever cloud its sunlit landscape.

Then again, this fairy tale is always seen in panorama, rarely in close-up shots. From such a distance, it proved enchanting. For decades, even birthmothers were blinded by its dazzle.

Religious organizations and adoption agencies owned this narrative. Early on, they declared, and nobody challenged them, that an adoptive family was exactly the same as a biological one! Exactly the same!! That a newborn could be grafted onto a family tree, and if it was done soon enough, nobody would ever be the wiser. With babies matched ethnically to the adopting parents, as was my son, nobody need ever know the secret. Nobody, including the baby, would ever know the difference!!

Until the latter decades of the 20th century, the disappeared mothers had no comment. They remained too afraid and ashamed to tell their stories.

Reality Bites

The adoption fairy tale could have been demolished back in the early 60's, as recounted in the archives of the University of Oregon's Adoption History Project. That's when Canadian social scientist H. David Kirk published the results of his years-long study of adoptive families. His book, *Shared Fate: A Theory of Adoption and Mental Health*, posits that transparency in adoption, the ability of adoptive parents and children to accept their "difference" from biological families, and to discard the secrets of closed adoption, resulted in families that were happier, healthier and emotionally stronger than those who kept the secrets. Children who were fully aware of their adoptive status, and of their new parents' infertility, were found to be able to be more resilient and happier than those trapped in family secrets.

Kirk was himself the adoptive father of four. He studied some 2,000 adoptive families, virtually all of them headed by infertile couples. As his work progressed, Kirk divided these families into two categories, those who rejected difference and those who embraced it, integrating the facts of adoption into their family story.

Kirk found that adopting other people's children did not ease the pain of infertility. Instead, the adoptive parents carried this pain with them into parenthood where it festered despite being deeply submerged in the family's daily life. The solution Kirk suggested was for adoptive parents and children to connect through their "shared fate" of familial loss and disconnection, either with or without the assistance of therapists.

Research since has confirmed and amplified many aspects of Kirk's study, most especially his assertion that adoptive families are different and require extra support based on transparency and truthfulness. Kirk's most cogent argument, well supported by recent research, is that adoption is a fragile form of kinship, fraught with emotional danger. But at the time, in the 60s, his theories did not jibe with those of adoption professionals in the United States who were determined uphold the fairy tale and their own powerful role in it. They insisted that Adoption Land as practiced, was a sunlit place full of promise: bastard babies were transformed into the loved offspring of new families and infertile couples achieved the golden dream of parenthood.

If Kirk's work had generated serious discussions among adoption agencies and clergy it might have exposed the win-win adoption fairy tale for the flimsy and treacherous thing it is. And many thousands of adoptive parents and adoptees might have been spared the emotional agonies that accompany the secrets of closed adoption. But that did not happen until decades later. Only in the '90s did adult adoptees en masse begin to demand knowledge of their biological identity and to tell the world what they needed but didn't get when they were growing up.

Sweet Fantasies

I n the early episodes of the Emmy-winning TV show *This Is Us,* Randall, the Sterling K. Brown character, an adoptee, reunites with the biological father who'd abandoned him as a newborn on the steps of a Pittsburgh fire station several decades before. The program beautifully depicts this highly charged, almost miraculous, reunion of the son with his now terminally ill first father William (played by Ron Cephas Jones).

Randall has used a private detective to track his father down.

"I am your biological son," Randall says simply when the older man opens the door to his humble apartment in a rundown building. The moment of reunion is both exquisite and heartbreaking.

In its aftermath, Randall and his father, an erstwhile poet, experience wild mood swings as the foundations of their lives shift and wobble. These upsets continue in later episodes as a tangle of betrayals and deceptions surrounding Randall's adoption are revealed. Which is exactly what happens in real life more often than not. Shifting. Wobbling. A realignment of all other personal relationships and the connections between present and past in the families.

In the television series, both men get stuck on the emotional roller coaster of reunion as they try to connect after a lifetime apart. Despite much confusion and many obstacles, they develop an intimacy and deep love for one another that may be the sweetest fantasy of all first parents and adult adoptees. (Both actors won Emmy awards for their work in these heart-wrenching roles.) Not surprisingly, however, the series leaves out the steps Randall must have taken leading up to his symphonic reunion with his father. It steers clear of any revelations about the rarity of such intimate and loving reconnections.

Reunion Redux

If my relationship with my relinquished son had blossomed into the kind shared by the characters in *This Is Us,* my story would be easier to understand. It might have been easier to write. But that is not what happened. In the immediate aftermath of our second disconnection, I spent a long time licking my wounds. I was hurt and confused. But that's also when I began to look into those hidden, mostly forgotten, places inside myself. A year or so after that, we re-reconnected.

In my distress I'd joined a post-adoption support group that included several male adult adoptees. They suggested that I needed to understand my son's own many losses: the mother who raised him, his brother, and his marriage. Plus his time in the military, his deployments during both Operation Desert Shield and Desert Storm. They convinced me that my surrendered son would want me to reach back out. With this in mind I emailed him and asked the simple question, do you want to try again? He said yes, and so we did.

Since then, our relationship has stopped and restarted several times. Writing about it is painful. I want to maintain my son's anonymity. (I've changed a couple of small details to help protect it. He didn't ask to be in my story, after all.) But I also have to be true to my own experience. Which means I have to include some interactions that strongly impacted it. While my son's birth and relinquishment are at the heart of my story, he, as he lives now, is only tangential to what I am writing. Which is the story of my unmarried pregnancy, coerced relinquishment, and an aftermath of life-changing loss concealed by a dark secret. The man my relinquished son has grown into has nothing to do with that, but I can't complete my story without examining our reconnection.

Our second reunion has not been easy. We live hundreds of miles apart. We communicate mostly via text, email, and phone calls. We have not broken through whatever it is that keeps us from connecting in an intimate way even though we've had two extended in person visits. Instead, we circle around the superficialities of our lived lives, seemingly unable to talk about the things that matter most to us. Or maybe it's just me.

In 2019 he came to New Jersey for several days. I put him up in a hotel nearby, not yet ready to host him in my home. We shared meals, went out to eat, walked my dog and talked a lot. The rest of my family – my daughters and my son-in-law, along with Dennis and Gabriel, joined us for dinner once or twice. I hauled out the MacDonnell family reunion books, revealing much about his genetic ancestry and his namesake Angus. He examined them but didn't comment that I recall.

The next year, at the height of the pandemic, he visited me at my summer rental in southern Vermont, near my youngest daughter's home. It was a big apartment in a ramshackle Victorian with a lovely backyard overlooking the Black River. During this time together, we again tried hard to connect. At various points my raised children joined us, including Marisa's life partner and their new baby, Lily, my second grandchild. Lots of good food, some home-cooked, and some ordered in. The pandemic dictated most of our movements but we had plenty of time alone together. We spent a lot of time in that backyard. But when he left Vermont for home he did not say good-bye. I realized he was gone only after I got up. I waited that day for a text acknowledging his exit, his safe arrival home, maybe a thank you, but I did not get one. I know I could be accused of "over mothering," or of inappropriate expectations.

But this odd disconnection was just one of many between us. It reminded me yet again that our relationship is essentially ambiguous. Maybe I was expecting him to behave as my raised children would have, responding to my request: Text me when you're home safe! But at the same time that he was my son, he was not my son. Did I have a right to expect anything from him?

As far back as he knew anything, my son knew that he'd been adopted; that his three siblings – two older, one younger – had been adopted too. These adoptions in his family were a fact but "not a big deal," he said. They were never dwelled upon. He'd always felt loved, he said. His family, with its heady aspirations, followed the complex mores of 20th century upper middle class Catholicism, one living close to the swirl of culture and politics in the nation's capital. (A well-run household with many rules and regulations, good behavior, good manners, and good grooming required at all times, mandatory religious education under the guiding eye of a Jesuit uncle.) A fine childhood, all in all, he said.

I was relieved and happy to learn this. How could I not be? I was comforted to know that he'd been well educated, that his health had been attended do, that he'd been given chances to dabble in many activities including athletics and the arts. He got to go to sleep-away camp every summer. Growing up, he went through all of the typical American rites of passage of his race and class. His new family was able to give him so many things that I could not, one of the true things drilled into me at St. Mary's Infant Asylum. That Dickensian vision survived inside me.

His mother was an elementary school teacher who retired once she became a mother. She was, in his telling, warm and loving, attentive and committed. His father was smart, strong and accomplished. A steadfast paterfamilias who is still living and still taking care of his family. (His father, like my own and my husband, had considered entering the priesthood before realizing he did not have a vocation after all. Like orphanhood and lost children, this attraction to the priesthood is a strange rhyme in my family.)

By his own account, my son was as ignorant as I about adoption reform. Happy in his family, he never paid attention to adoption matters. He knew nothing about adoption reform. His adoptive family may have belonged in the category that researcher David Kirk labeled "rejection of difference," the holy grail of the adoption movement in the United States.

When he learned years after the fact that Massachusetts had opened its adoption records (never mind that birth parents were not informed) he sent a check for $25 along with the proper identification to the Suffolk County bureau of vital statistics. Weeks later that document, his original birth certificate, showed up in his mailbox. After that, he said, it took him about 15 minutes to find me online. Hence, he said he never experienced the anguish of countless other adoptees who spend their lives, and many thousands of dollars, often in futility, to locate their genetic roots. His search, by his own account, was easy peasy. I told him about my own abortive attempts to find my own sealed records, and the anguish it had caused me.

During his first New Jersey visit I asked him, prompted by my own curiosity, what his parents told their children about the women whose children they'd adopted. They must have said something, I prodded when he hesitated.

"No judgments," he answered, a phrase that has stayed with me. No judgments. He said it more than once and that is all he has ever said to me about the birth mothers who made his family possible.

But judgments, harsh negative judgments, had been in the air for decades by then. Everyone everywhere was familiar with those judgments. If there were, as he claims, "no judgments" in his family, he is also acknowledging that judgments had indeed been made, early and often. Unwed mothers existed in a slagheap of detrimental judgments. Perhaps they'd been considered in his family and then discarded because his good family refused to allow them. Or maybe they believed it was God's will that they became the parents of these particular children.

Back before I gave birth, my caseworker had promised me that my baby, gender as yet unknown, would be the first child in his new family! With the smidgeon of agency that I had, I'd asked for this. I wanted my baby to be special, the star of a new family: Number One! I didn't want him placed in a family that was as crowded as mine had been with close in age siblings and a stay-at-home mother who was always overburdened.

I felt so betrayed, yet again by my caseworker, when I learned, from my son, that he was the third child placed in his family! That he already had two sisters, and that a brother would join them very soon. Even after all this time, this betrayal stings.

This wasn't my caseworker's only prevarication. She also told me, or maybe she merely allowed me to believe, that my baby, taken from my arms in that hospital corridor, was heading straight to his new family. Not so. He went instead to a temporary foster home, then a more permanent foster home, until he was settled in with his new family at about three months old. (Until I signed the "termination of parental rights" I was charged $15 a week for his care. My parents made sure to collect it.) He had at least four caregivers in his first weeks of life.

Caseworkers, I've learned since from other mothers of adoption loss, lied routinely to birth mothers. They felt no obligation to be honest. Instead, given court-imposed secrecy, they were confident that their mendacity would never be discovered. They'd say anything to speed the baby through the adoption process and complete the placement.

Hence, the countless transactions of closed adoption are riddled with deceptions and misinformation. Those who knew the most, birth mothers, were not allowed into the conversation. Our truths have come out only slowly from researchers and birth mother memoirists who insist on telling their truth, one that subverts the official story.

My intuition tells me that my son grew up in the bubble of the win-win adoption fairy tale. That his new parents were dreamers of the golden adoption dream and they had the resources to make their dream come true. As far as I can tell, they stepped into their parental roles as surely as if they were the progenitors of their children. They'd waited so long!! Four kids, after years of infertility! A mind-boggling commitment of love and money. A family created by Catholic Charities that basked in the miracle of it.

I believe my son holds this story close: the chosen child, the heroic parents.

Whatever his parents told him when he was growing up is the story he has lived with all his life. The key plot point, despite his declaration of "no judgments" is that he had been "given up," i.e. discarded, and that the mother who did this was likely unstable if not dangerous. There is just no getting around the fact of such a relinquishment.

Having been unwanted is the root cause pulled out time and again when adoptees are told of their adoption, even though their first mothers are silenced and unavailable to correct the record. It's so easy to understand and believe this story. With its clash of good and bad, it's all but irresistible. It makes the adoptive parents more lovable, heroic even, and the first mother unworthy if not feckless. I have tried to dispel such ideas in my adopted son, to insist that he was loved from the moment of conception. I don't believe I have convinced him.

I do not in any way wish to intrude upon you and your life …other than to say thank you for having me…

I would love to hear from you at least to confirm you are my birth mother but again your life is your own.

In the years since I first read these words in my son's first email, I've often pondered them. I see things now that I, in my rush to reconnect, did not see at first. The language is polite and formal, cool, if not cold. Although the email is addressed directly to me, he refers to me as "one Julia MacDonnell." I stumbled on these words the first time I read them and every time since. It's an odd locution, never used in ordinary discourse; not one I'd expect in an email sent directly to me. One Julia MacDonnell – like a trespass for which I should be held accountable.

Moreover, he "suspected" that he'd found the "right" person, not that he'd hoped he'd found her or wanted to find her or had been looking for her, this woman, this "one Julia MacDonnell." The "right" person, who happened to his biological mother, the one named on his OBC. The woman who'd carried him and birthed him under the most inauspicious circumstances. If he felt warmth or excitement or a yearning for a connection with me he kept it well hidden.

I do not in any way wish to intrude...

To intrude means to put oneself into a situation or a place where one is neither expected nor welcome. It's both deliberate and uninvited. He tempers this by saying he does not "in any way wish" to intrude, and yet he goes ahead and intrudes. He knew he was intruding, and did it anyway. This suggests to me that he believed that it was his prerogative to intrude, that he had a right to. Which of course undermines his declaration, "your life is your own." My son evidently misapprehended the nature of his "intrusion'" and its possible impact on the "one Julia MacDonnell," me, who gave birth to him. He wrote as if our reconnection was no more than a quasi-legal transaction; as if the woman he was contacting, his first mother, would have no feelings about being "found" after almost 50 years of court-imposed silence. He expressed no apparent empathy for the person who'd just realized, via his email "intrusion," that the long-standing court-sealed document around which she (and her first family) had woven their secrets, was no longer in force.

It must not have occurred to him that she didn't know that Massachusetts had opened its closed adoption records without telling birth parents, a breath taking lapse by the state. Or maybe he didn't care one way or the other. Maybe it never occurred to him that women who relinquish children to adoption, never again fully own their lives. A piece of their soul has been ripped out. They're crimped ever after by life-long loss.

But back when I first opened his email, jubilation swamped every other feeling. In my rush to reconnect I picked up my phone and called him.

Are You My Mother?

Our reconnection has been, even in its best moments, a troubled one. Every one of our visits and conversation has been lashed by conflicting loyalties, confusing expectations, many of them unacknowledged, and that neither of us understand. I've often felt that everything I said and did in his presence was being measured against the stories he'd been told, or not told, when he was growing up. Or maybe against the mother who had raised him. Maybe that's why I preferred to have others around when I was with him, especially my children. Others provided some insulation, so I could remain grounded in myself, a reminder of who I am, not who I used to be.

Of course I wanted something from him every time we talked or met. I wanted something though at first I wasn't sure what it was. (Hidden expectations, the wrecking ball in so many relationships.) What I wanted in this reunion, I understand now, is acceptance and understanding, respect if not love. I didn't want to be his mother. It was too late for that. But I wanted him to understand the love I'd always felt for him. And I wanted some validation of my experience of relinquishment, the way I'd been manipulated into it, and an acknowledgement of its devastation to me.

Maybe my son wanted something similar from me but he never said so. Perhaps he wanted the missing piece in the puzzle of his life, although he has never suggested to me that a piece was missing. Curiosity, he has always maintained, was his driving motivation.

Several times in our conversations, perhaps exasperated by my leaning toward the past, he has said, "What's done is done; it can't be changed." He doesn't understand that for those who have been shattered by an experience, what's done is never done. It must be understood before any healing can begin.

In my sadness over our distressing reunion and my desire to make it better, I've reached out to my fellow CUB member, the therapist Leslie Pate Mackinnon. I've asked her many questions about reunion in adoption, trying to gain some insight into my own. We've never had a therapist/client relationship and I never explained the specifics of my own reunion. Nevertheless, in phone calls, emails, zoom meet-ups and in person at CUB's annual retreats, I've picked her brain about reunion in adoption and Mackinnon has always answered me fully and thoughtfully. For me, her decades of lived experience – her status as the first mother of two sons lost to adoption and then found, and as the mother of two raised children – give her special insight into the joys and hazards of reunion.

In order to quantify the magnitude of a reunion, Mackinnon argues, its participants – the searcher and the searched – must first understand, "the staggering degree of the original loss." This conviction is the foundation of her private practice and her national conference presentations. Only after my son found me did I begin to grasp just how staggering my original loss had been. Before that I'd lived so deeply in the fog that I didn't understand anything.

If Mackinnon had her way, every reunion in adoption would be carried out with "sensitive understanding" of the intra- and interpersonal dynamics that are bound to be stirred up. That's because, she points out, current research documents the "life-long consequences suffered by an infant abruptly severed from its mother following birth." (Those in the adoption reform community call this "the primal wound.") Likewise, research confirms, "the emotional cost to the mother, following the same, abrupt separation." For both mother and child, she says, "Developmental processes were interrupted and some may get reawakened during the reunion."

Preparation and education, Mackinnon believes, greatly enhance the chances for a successful reunion. Likewise, offering some structure and ground rules to the person being contacted can help reduce the thunderbolt of that first reconnection (i.e. his first email to me.) These prerequisites are "often overlooked," she said, especially when DNA test results are involved, in "the rush of excitement to fulfill a long held dream of meeting again."

The opening of sealed adoption records, not DNA results, enabled our reunion. Nevertheless, that "rush of excitement," a profound longing, set the pace for me. I grasped for contact though I had neither preparation nor education, no structure or ground rules. As a result, I've foundered in confusion and misery.

Mackinnon's final words: "Going slowly, with guidance towards considered and careful communication, is imperative."

Ironically enough, the preparation and structure Mackinnon speaks of are often available now through the same institutions that were complicit in creating the secrets of closed adoption in the first place: adoption agencies, family courts and state agencies. The structures and preparation are being developed in response to the crush of adult adoptees who (often through DNA testing) began demanding to know their genetic heritage at the end of the 20th and beginning of the 21st centuries.

These days, many open record states offer procedures for "confidential intermediaries" to serve as go-betweens for searchers and their targets. These confidential intermediaries (CIs) work on behalf of searchers. They are trained by the courts or adoption agencies to ease the potential shocks and wounds of reunion. Some are professional and some are volunteers but reaching out to the target to explain that a lost family member is hoping for contact.

Those being "searched for" can take whatever time they need to decide what next step to take or if they do not wish to take any. (Only adult adoptees, those over 18 years old, are able to participate.) The CI does not reveal names or contact information between the parties but may offer advice about how to navigate the first meeting. Often, the searcher and target exchange letters via the CI before they meet in person, often with the CI present.

Even so, not all first mothers, and not all adoptees, wish to meet.

The process may go on for months or years. By the time a mediated first meeting takes place, both parties, under the guidance of the CI, not only understand the nature of the transaction, but they also know important things about one another and their own expectations. The point is to enable an honest, peaceful and possibly openhearted reunion if its participants so wish.

Passages

By the time my first son got in touch with me, my long marriage, despite our efforts at conflict resolution, was coming to an end, mostly, I see now, as the result of our never mourned losses, his and mine. Navigating a difficult grown up world, with little emotional or financial support from family, required more than we had the resources to deal with. Deep and unresolvable disagreements about what we wanted out of life, what we could give up and what we couldn't, and how we wanted to raise our children, made it healthier for us to live apart.

We also endured some rare stresses during our marriage. Dennis's brother, after waiting a decade for his number to come up in the federal immigration lottery, moved with his pregnant wife and son from the Fiji Islands to our town in New Jersey. We served as sponsors for their emigration and welcomed them with open arms. We also took on the tasks of settling the family into their new lives in the United States. We found homes, health care, job training and jobs for them; childcare and schools for the kids. I did endless amounts of childcare.

Not long after their arrival, I was diagnosed with breast cancer and survived a mastectomy and harsh chemotherapy. Six weeks after my diagnosis, my loved sister Veronica was diagnosed with ovarian cancer. She lived for three more years, enduring countless surgeries, radiation and chemotherapy. We were bald together. She died at 50, survived by her husband and sons, and leaving a crater in my life and that of my children.

My parents had divorced in the late 70s after my mother's feminist awakening. She left him. My father tried but failed to get an annulment for his marriage to my mother on the grounds that she was mentally ill. He remarried; my mother did not. Ma died in 1990, Daddy a decade later. Each left behind messes regarding their estates. Daddy's second wife, for example, sued his estate (inherited by his children) for more money than he'd left her, a litigation that dragged on for years. I saw both parents' post-death tumult as a result of their life-long denials and refusals, not to mention how they, unknowingly or not, pitted their children against each other.

After all that, I was waiting for, and believing in, the peaceful period promised to aging women who have worked hard enough at their own lives. I'm not sure why, but I thought it had been promised and I also thought I'd worked hard enough. Then my first son found me.

What's Done Is Never Done

After my son and I re-reconnected, I again tried to get my file from Catholic Charities of the Archdiocese of Boston. I had no idea what it might contain or if it would answer any of my questions, especially my questions about the termination of my parental rights. I'd never be at peace until I saw it. Lo and behold! After I mailed them a copy of my son's original birth certificate, and a notarized statement that we had reconnected, along with another $25 check, they found my file! In April 2019 the manila envelope showed up in my mailbox: first class mail, sent via the USPS for $1.90. On the envelope, the Catholic Charities logo, a misshapen heart with a cross inside. Catholic Charities, Laboure Center, South Boston.

Why does it matter after all this time? I asked myself before I sent for it and again after I opened it. It's a question I'd also asked myself many times before. Why does it matter after all this time? Perhaps the great essayist Leslie Jamison was wrong when she declared that *female pain is always news; we've never heard it all before.*

Even the man whose birth it documents has advised me, more than once, to *let it go,* to let the past stay in the past. I think he'd prefer for me to do that. He'd prefer to stay out of the tangled weeds of how his identity was "amended" in the first few weeks of his life as he experienced a flurry of caregivers. But I can't. Excavating and understanding my own experience matters more than anything, a promise that I might, in these records, find the parts of myself I lost during that dark time.

The envelope is stuffed with blurry hard copies. These date back to the early days of xerography. No electronic files from the Baby Scoop!! Among them is another birth mother's request for non-identifying information about her surrendered son! How did this crucial top-secret document end up in my file? (Did she ever find her son? Did he ever find her?) So much for the sanctity of Catholic Charities' records.

On the top of the pile is my son's "amended" birth certificate. It's just a piece of paper but a potent one, the one that changes his identity, steals from him his genetic history, the document over which acrimonious legislative battles in many states continue to be waged.

This "amended" birth certificate shows my son's new name and erases mine along with my experience. (He was named after a loved member of his extended adoptive family as I'd named him after one in mine.) This document identifies only his adoptive parents. It signals his new life in his new family. By the time this one was filed, my son was six months old and his family had left Massachusetts for good.

As I looked at it, rage and sorrow churned inside me. It's one thing to know a document exists. It's another thing to hold it in your hands and see the state-sanctioned erasure of reality and the permanent loss of a son. I closed the envelope. Months passed before I was able to look at it again.

During the dark winter of 2020 when the Covid-19 pandemic radically altered everyday life, I retrieved that envelope from the closet where I'd stuck it. I studied its contents. If I hadn't been sheltering in place, alone, I might not have done it. If I hadn't had my raised children close by, and had I not taught and reread Louise DeSalvo's brilliant craft book *Writing as a Way of Healing* a million times, I might not have been able to do it. Because its contents reveal in printed words an even darker experience than the one I'd repressed for most of my life.

Among official records pertaining to my son's birth weight, etc., it also contained pages of handwritten and typed notes about me by my caseworker Gail Murray, my counselor "Jackie" at the home, and the woman I've called Hannah at whose home I sometimes spent weekends and holidays. These notes, with me as the focus, include correspondence among them. These notes are initialed, not signed. I could see the faces of these women clearly but, at first, I couldn't remember their names.

Eventually those names floated up out of the umbra and I googled them. Two are still living in the Boston area. But my caseworker, Gail Kirker Murray, has passed on. Vivid memories of her, the pretend friend my parents loved. She was thin and plain, with a pious, missionary edge. In 1967 she was just starting out in her social work career but she proved, through the rest of the century, to be very good at what she did. She went on to a stellar career taking babies from their mothers, uncounted numbers of them, though she never had any of her own. Eventually she would become a regional director of Catholic Family Services, lauded for her competence in matching bastard infants to new families. In the Fall 1984 newsletter of Catholic Family Services, Murray is photographed standing beside Bernard Francis Law, the cardinal who, in 2002, would resign in disgrace for covering up the sexual abuse of children by priests under his administration in Boston. The newsletter is celebrating a gala fundraising dinner for the archdiocese's work with mothers and children.

What these women wrote about me shoved me back into the darkest of dark places, a place I didn't believe still existed inside of me until I found out, ever so shockingly, that it did. It was a place of despair where I was not merely misunderstood but looked down upon as a kind of miscreant to be studied like a lab specimen.

This file, with its bedraggled blurry photocopies, became my book of revelation, an emphatic confirmation of the flimsy intuitions I'd had back when it was going on. They offered a window through which I could see, in the eerie light of the past, how others saw me all those decades ago. And I saw what I'd always felt: how vulnerable and discard-able I'd been.

The first time I read their handwritten notes, their words transformed me into a banshee, shrieking and spinning out my rage and anguish. But eventually, after many readings, I calmed down. I saw things I'd never been able to see before. Empathy was not among them. My shame clarified. I began to understand how, when I was still a teenager, I'd been immersed in a shame so profound, so toxic, and so viscous, that I never again felt unstained. This experience of shame, and my fear of experiencing it again, became the foundation of my adult self.

My intake evaluation misspells my given name and my surname. It identifies me as "Julie McDonald." Maybe that's a small mistake but it feels like a big one. Nobody cared enough to get it right. It describes me as a "factory worker." And it's true, the summer of my pregnancy, 1966, I did work in a factory. But I was never a factory worker in the true meaning of that word, a lifelong laborer within factory walls. I was an honor student, a brainy girl, ordered by my father into the factory for a temporary summer job.

Several times in these notes they describe me as moderately attractive. For example: "She is at this point only moderately attractive." Only! This evaluation plunged me back into the dark heart of my family where I was deemed neither as pretty nor as thin as my sisters. These certified members of the Unholy Trinity repeat this description several times with variations – *moderately attractive but unkempt;' moderately attractive but of at least above average intelligence.*

My looks, my being "only moderately attractive" or "at best moderately attractive" seemed to be of paramount importance to these women and another trespass for which I should do penance. Why? I still can't fathom it.

But "unkempt" is an outright lie. I happen to be obsessive about personal hygiene and grooming. I'm rarely even unkempt when I climb into bed. My kids joke about how I have to "put on my face," lipstick, mascara and blush, before I step outside the door to get the mail or walk the dog.

What did these women see? I wondered as I read their evaluations. What were they looking at? My homemade clothes? The zits on my chin? My DIY haircut, pulled into a ponytail? My poverty? Chances are I was shabby in hand-sewn or hand-me-down clothes. I didn't have a dime to spend on myself, but unkempt? Never.

They also write that I kept my room in a 'deplorable' condition. How could this be, I wondered. I had nothing of my own, no possessions with me except my few clothes and some books. How much of a mess could I have made? *Deplorable.*

I realize it's irrational that such words bother me fifty years after they were written, but they do. They slash deep. My anger and sense of injustice about my treatment came roaring back.

I recall my times with these women only vaguely, a break from the tedium of daily life at the home. I glimpse myself, my sad shabby self, so naïve, talking to them as if they were the trusted confidants they presented themselves to be. Dependent upon them to get me through whatever was coming next, I answered their questions. Perhaps I confided, though silent self-preservation was my M.O. throughout my stay, and maybe for the rest of my life.

Reading their notes, I realized, as I'd always suspected, that they shared whatever I told them with each other and my parents – my parents quoted back to me their assessments and used them to berate me or punish me. Holding in my hands their ancient writing I'm again scorched by betrayal, a feeling that undermined forever my ability to trust anyone with power over me.

Reading their notes, I feel again their condescension; their veiled contempt. I see how, so sure of themselves, (and yet so laughably clueless to contemporary eyes) they pinged off one another, reiterating and enhancing my shortcomings, my failings, and my unworthiness to become a mother.

To them I was little more than a specimen, something to be objectively studied and then discarded. Case closed.

It's clear they were using the prevailing Gladney-Bernstein playbook, replete with its wild assumptions and erroneous perceptions, to prove that I wasn't fit to raise a child. This made it easier for them to take my baby.

Two particular passages released other memories from the umbra. My caseworker wrote that I was hospitalized for a week because I'd gained too much weight, not for the pregnancy health crisis of preeclampsia. They wrote that I had to be confined to bed rest and IV fluids in order to lose weight! I couldn't sneak food while confined to a hospital bed! Weight gain, is what my caseworker wrote in my file, all the better to portray me as slothful, perhaps committing the sin of gluttony, and unable to care for myself. (Excess weight had always been deemed an awful failure in my family. Chubby children deserved ridicule.)

All these decades later, the book of revelation also solves the mystery of why I was separated from my baby for the 48 hours after his birth and why the delivery room was draped in white as I, the apparent locus of filth, was wheeled out of it. The doctor thought I might have gonorrhea! For reasons known only to himself, maybe just because he could, he sent my vaginal secretions to the lab to be tested before they would allow me near my baby. The test results required 48 hours.

Reading this, I am confounded, almost nauseous. I feel again, in excruciating ways, the loss of those two days post-partum. I can't stop trembling and again I have to put the file away. Why would they think I might have gonorrhea? I'd been monitored all but obsessively at their clinic since August with no signs of any STD. Throughout my prenatal care, I understood that they were more interested in the baby's health than in mine, but time and again they declared me extremely healthy. I was, after all, giving birth to a blue-ribbon baby, the prized bastard of a healthy educated middle class white girl. Likewise, when I was hospitalized, I was given every possible test. No symptoms ever of any STD. Furthermore, I had no history of promiscuity, as they well knew from their incessant questioning. And the baby's father was a clean-cut college boy. Never mind any of that. The idea of me suffering from gonorrhea was irresistible, a crucial plot point in their narrative of the sick slutty teenager who was not fit to be a mother.

Early on, my counselor Jackie wrote, "It is my impression that this girl is and has been in the throes of adolescent reaction. The depression and acting out of it is almost classical." Almost classical! Who knew? But neither she nor anyone else ever explained any of that to me, nor offered any help for my depression. Nor is there any evidence in my file that she or anyone else ever wondered why, as she noted, that I was a "first-class actor-outer." They wanted my baby and once they had him they were done with me.

At the end of my intake report for St. Mary's Infant Asylum is an action plan. There it is, in printed words: "placement planning" for my baby, a plan made for me but without me. This must have happened in meetings, letters, or phone conversations among the members of the trinity when I was too scared, confused and immature to understand that I had a right to join the conversation. A conversation I didn't even know was going on. I was too scared to question anything. The book of revelation confirms what I'd always felt: I never took part in the decision to give up my baby.

Cultural Kerfuffle

In 1992, around the time that adult adoptees *en masse* began agitating for access to their original birth certificates and the pain of birth mothers was first identified in social science research, a popular sitcom expressed in comedic fashion the changing mores of that time. Murphy Brown, the mouthy protagonist of that eponymous Emmy – winning sitcom, gets pregnant at 42. Candice Bergen played the unmarried TV news anchor. In a move deemed edgy at the time, she decides to keep her baby. With television viewing still confined to the three major networks, it's estimated that 38 million people tuned in to watch the childbirth episode. In it, a joyful Murphy, after giving birth, sings to her baby a chorus of the Aretha Franklin hit, *I Feel Like a Natural Woman.*

As it happened, Bergen, in real life, was pregnant by her real life husband, the French director Louis Malle, and would soon give birth to their daughter Chloe. Hence, Murphy Brown's TV pregnancy was an accommodation by the show-runners to Bergen's actual condition rather than an unprecedented feminist statement. By the time Murphy Brown had her baby, legal abortion had been available for at least two decades, along with safe and reliable contraception. Given the wild popularity of the program, its producers must have assumed it was safe to step into the turbulent waters of female reproductive choice.

But Murphy's reproductive choice turned out to be intensely polarizing, as if the show runners had deliberately lobbed a Molotov cocktail into the heart of the culture. They failed to see that Murphy's choice teetered near that abyss where women got to control their own fertility and decide on their own when to become mothers. Making matters worse, Murphy Brown's brash personality and professional success challenged the abiding American concept of motherhood: chaste, docile and all giving.

The episode, surprisingly or not, triggered fierce denunciations, revealing that female fertility, despite the recent gains in reproductive choice, remained as politically charged as it had ever been.

Vice President Dan Quayle, stumping in San Francisco as part of George H. W. Bush's unsuccessful quest for reelection, got into the act. In a move that today would no doubt go viral, he accused Murphy Brown of mocking "the importance of fathers by bearing a child alone and calling it just another lifestyle choice."

Using scorched earth rhetoric, Quayle declared that Murphy Brown's unmarried motherhood signaled the disintegration of America's family values. He went so far as to equate it with the Los Angeles riots that had just ravaged South Central Los Angeles. Sixty-eight people were killed in those riots and 2,000 more were injured.

The day after Quayle's speech, the New York Daily News ran this front-page headline: *Quayle to Murphy Brown: 'You Tramp.'* What Quayle and the Daily News editors seemed to have forgotten was that Murphy Brown was only a fictional character.

Feminists, myself included, thought Quayle's proclamations were ridiculous, the lamentations of a loser. He didn't understand how times had changed. But others and I failed to see that Quayle's outrage about Murphy's choice was more than hyperbolic rhetoric. It was a harbinger: his seemingly laughable commentary was the surface ripple of a deep and abiding current, one that has regained power in the decades since. It's the current that demolished, in a terrifying wave, the constitutional right to an abortion, and is now curtailing reproductive choice in so many states. It's the same old patriarchal, quasi-religious forces determined to control female fertility, the same players who denigrated unwed mothers back in the day and took their babies. They deem control of female fertility God-given to the righteous.

Soon after the Murphy Brown kerfuffle, on the opposite side of the country, and after nearly a century of operation, St. Mary's Infant Asylum closed its doors. The adjacent St. Margaret's Hospital also closed. Unwed mothers no longer required sequestration and the mission of the lying-in hospital may have been deemed too costly, or just redundant. Whatever the reason, the nuns departed, controversially moving the operations of the hospital to a more prosperous neighborhood in Brighton. St. Margaret's Lying In Hospital was transformed into a pavilion of the massive St. Elizabeth's Medical Center.

Not long after that, bulldozers rolled in to demolish the infant asylum. That elaborate, century old Georgian mansion collapsed into its own basement, in an explosion of brick, glass, wood, dust, unidentified debris and millions of memories. The weeping of the mothers who'd passed through its doors and left without their babies could not be heard above the din. Nor could the cries of those countless relinquished babies sent out into the world and their new families.

The hospital building was not demolished. Over the coming years, it was renovated and converted into the St. Mary's Center for Women and Children, a non-profit agency that, by its own account, was created to help "women and children who have experienced trauma and are living in poverty." It is partially funded by the Archdiocese of Boston.

The St. Mary's Center web page claims to support about 600 young mothers and babies every year with "shelter, clinical and educational services, job training, employment placement, and the search for affordable permanent housing."

Wow! I thought when I read this. Now this facility, instead of taking babies from their mothers, gives young mothers, almost all of them women of color, the resources they need to keep and raise their children!! What could be more wonderful? I hope it's true.

Yet the historical time line presented on St. Mary's website is troubling. The St. Mary's Center declares its mission as continuing "a rich history of caring for young mothers and their children," that was first established by the Daughters of Charity in 1870. Although the physical location of St. Mary's changed several times during that century and a half, the website states that its mission has stayed the same: "welcoming pregnant and parenting teen girls and their infants, and providing them with shelter, comfort, and care."

Imagine how startled I was by this alluring declaration: comfort and care. To prove its point, the website offers a timeline of its operations titled "A Journey Through Time":

1870: An infant is left on the steps of St. James' Church in Boston's South End and is taken in by the Daughters of Charity at Carney Hospital… St. Ann's Ward is established …to provide shelter, comfort, and care for other abandoned babies.

1874: St. Ann's Ward at Carney Hospital had already cared for over 1,500 infants and 300 unwed mothers. With the growing demand for services for women and children, St. Mary's Infant Asylum and Lying-in Hospital is established in a mansion on Bowdoin Street in Dorchester.

1894: Following an outpouring of compassion and generosity from the community, St. Mary's purchases the Green estate on Jones Hill in Dorchester and moves operations to St. Mary's current location near Upham's Corner.

1902: By this year, more than 1,000 infants and unwed mothers call St. Mary's home. The babies have been abandoned or abused, and at that time, the young mothers were likely to have been cast out of their homes with nowhere else to turn.

1929: As the demand for services becomes greater, St. Mary's expands into a general hospital, incorporating itself as St. Margaret's

Hospital. Medical facilities are added onto the original building and a nurse-training program is established.

1943: As the hospital continues to expand, the facility can no longer accommodate the hundreds of orphaned children at St. Mary's Infant Asylum. As a result, children are moved to boarding homes, leaving only infants on the St. Margaret's Hospital campus.

1993: All operations of St. Margaret's Hospital are moved from Dorchester to the Women's Health Pavilion at St. Elizabeth's Medical Center in Brighton. St. Mary's continues the legacy first established by the Daughters of Charity at St. Ann's Ward in 1870, welcoming pregnant and parenting teen girls and their infants, and providing them with shelter, comfort, and care.

This timeline of St. Mary's, through its several iterations, reflects the arc of history: the dire poverty and lack of social safety nets for mothers and babies in the decades after the Civil War and all the way up to the pre- and post-war years of the 20th century. The numbers are staggering: a thousand mothers and babies resided there in 1902! A hospital and nursing school were established to handle the demand! By 1943, orphaned children, having overwhelmed the facility, are moved into area boarding homes!

This last is shocking. Perhaps the removal of the older orphans refers to the beginning of today's foster case system. But I can't help worrying about the quality of childcare in these "boarding homes," and noting that the babies who "aged out" were also "cast out." How old were they when this happened?

But the most troubling thing is that half-century long lapse in the timeline. What happened at St. Mary's during the decades between 1943 and 1993 before that old mansion was demolished? Not one word! No mention of newborn adoption, no explanation of compelled secrecy, court-sealed documents, or of the well-defined process of shaming by which they wrested newborns from their mothers' arms.

The entire Baby Scoop Era is erased! No tally of how many babies were taken from their resource-less mothers and handed off to well-heeled couples. No tally of how many of mothers and babies were, like me, devastated by the experience. Rather, we were surgically removed from history.

Whoomp! There It Is!

A fter all my decades of doubt and wondering, it was right there in the file, the signed surrender of my parental rights. At last I'd come to it, the end of a long journey, my personal trail of tears.

Catholic Charitable Bureau of Boston, Inc.
Archdiocese of Boston

AGREEMENT FOR ADOPTION

For and in consideration of expenses incurred or to be incurred by the Catholic Charitable Bureau of Boston, Inc., duly incorporated under the laws of Massachusetts:

In behalf of my child............Angus John MacDonnell............now in charge of said Institution and to enable its managers to procure for...........him...........a suitable home in a good family where...........he...........may be adopted as a member properly provided for and educated, I do hereby delegate to them my authority over...........him...........and I do of my own free will give ....him...........up to them for the purpose of legal adoption or such other disposition as may be approved by them as best for...........his...........welfare and I do hereby surrender, fully and unreservedly, said child and give...........him...........to the Catholic Charitable Bureau of Boston, Inc. agreeing that I will neither seek to discover...........his...........home, attempt...........his...........removal therefrom nor in any way molest the family in which...........he...........may be placed or other parties interested.

In witness whereof, this paper having been first read to me, I have hereunto set my hand at............Lynn, Massachusetts............this............twenty-fourth............day of............January............19 67

In presence of

Subscribed and sworn to before me
this............24th............day of............January, 1967

NOTARY PUBLIC

PARENT
OF
SAID CHILD

This particular piece of paper is unlike any I have seen online, documents required by various states posted for the curious on the Internet. No government issued this one. Instead, it bears the official insignia of the Catholic Charitable Bureau of Boston, Inc., the Archdiocese of Boston. It's not even called a permanent termination of parental rights. Rather, it's labeled an 'agreement for adoption.'

This ancient document burns my hands like battery acid. I see my own signature there at the bottom. The sight of it, little changed in the decades since, sweeps my legs out from under me. It kills off my long held suspicion that my son's adoption was illegal. No grace period. No turning back.

"I do of my own free will give him up …for the purpose of legal adoption or such other disposition as may be approved … as best for his welfare and I do hearby surrender, fully and unreservedly, said child and give him to the Catholic Charitable Bureau of Boston, Inc., agreeing that I will neither seek to discover his home, attempt his removal therefrom nor in any way attempt to molest the family in which he may be placed or other parties interested."

This termination of my parental rights, with its archaic language, seems to imply possible criminality. No wonder it triggered the intense fear my failed search created within me. Any wonder I'd absolutely repressed my memories of it?

This document is dated Jan. 24, 1967, three weeks after I gave birth. Did I even read it before signing it? I don't remember. If I had, I doubt I would have understood the language. Even now, the words defy comprehension. What other "such disposition" might have been approved? "Molest" the family? I can hardly bear to think of it.

Yet the document I hold is not judicial. It has no apparent connection to any court but rather to the Catholic Church. It is a Diocese of Boston document. How did this happen, in a nation that claims to cherish the separation of church and state? How did the church obtain the power to take babies from their mothers? To decide which families got created and which were destroyed?

Even more shocking: It's my mother, not my father, who signed as one of the two required witnesses! This fact stupefies me as much as the document itself. My mother's unmistakable signature! Right there on that ancient page. The second signer is, of course, my caseworker, Gail Kirker Murray.

I have trouble processing that it was my mother, not my father, who drove me to the appointment to sign my son's surrender papers. After all, she'd shunned me throughout my ordeal. She'd ignored me and/or denigrated me. Never said a kind word or offered a whiff of empathy.

I stare at this paper, the surrender of my parental rights, transfixed. I hope it will trigger at least some small memory of the signing. I stare and stare. Only one tiny shard floats up: We are going to a suburban office, not to a court-house. Even so, my self-created conspiracy theories notwithstanding, my son's adoption was legal, after all. I did, in fact, sign away my rights to him three weeks after I gave birth to him.

Gazing into the spectral light of my past, I understand that, at that moment, in that place and time, January 24, 1967, I wasn't capable of doing anything of my own free will, and certainly not of surrendering, fully and unre-servedly, my baby. Anyone who thought I was, among them, my parents, my caseworker and all the priests and nuns, must have been delusional. By then, my will, my inner strength, had been tormented out of me even though I had no language to describe it, no language for what was happening. I couldn't for-mulate any thoughts or feelings about it. I was a ghost, swept into something far more powerful than my wounded teen-age self could understand.

There I was, three weeks post-partum, still bleeding. I did not have my baby though my body, my mind and heart contained his birth and loss. I had loved him (gender unknown, but correctly intuited) deeply in utero. I talked to him and sang to him and danced with him. I held him, my arms around my own big belly, hoping he could hear me and feel my love. But he was gone. I did not have him, an emptiness and longing so profound I cannot describe it. Three weeks post-partum. Three weeks since Gail Kirker Murray had taken him away, charging me $15 a week for his care until his adoption could be finalized. I don't know where she took him. I was not privy to that information. Silence and secrets already seethed.

During these three weeks, nobody had acknowledged my physical condition or emotional pain. This last, emotional pain, did not exist in my family. Feelings were not allowed. Hence, our family life was business as usual, one big 'happy' family, perfect on the outside. *Nothing to see here.* My parents set up a temporary bedroom for me, in the tiny TV room off our kitchen. To have put me back into the basement bedroom I shared with my sister would likely have resulted in the serious maiming or death of one of us. Otherwise, I was left to cope on my own.

Our trip to Lynn for the signing of that document would have been a daylong journey, Lynn being 50 miles from our Plainville home. Another trip across the city. Surprising that Ma would have taken on the task. We were rarely alone together. She'd never had any patience for me and by then she could hardly bear the sight of me.

Ma had always been a nervous driver. Her fingers twitched and tapped around the steering wheel as her right foot jerked from brake and to gas pedal and back again. By the time I was an adolescent I'd been in two crashes with her, one serious, the other not so much. But there she was, driving me to the far side of Boston to sign away my rights to my baby, her first grandchild.

For months I ponder this. Why did Ma, not Daddy, take me? Drifting off to troubled sleep one night, I figured it out: Daddy had chickened out. After all of the cruelties he'd visited upon me, he couldn't handle chauffeuring me to the office where I'd give up my child, his grandson, Angus John MacDonnell. He, the devoted if misguided paterfamilias, was riddled with unacknowledged contradictions. His whole life he was hobbled by his refusal to know himself, an affliction my parents shared. So, no, he could not sign as a witness. Daddy left my mother holding the bag, as he so often did. Ma had no similar reservations, no doubts, and no second thoughts. She'd said over and over again, as if it were a tragic and incomprehensible fate, that she refused to become a grandmother at 40. Only low class people did that, and she had married up, up, up. She was not low class, a description she'd been fighting her whole life. If it meant she had to waste a day driving to Lynn with her brat of a daughter, so be it. She'd put an end to this mess once and for all.

No memories of this event or of the days immediately before or after. Nobody was interested in me, in my condition, so I kept it to myself. I shoved it into the umbra, that queer unlighted place deep inside myself. It's a struggle to go back there, even in my imagination. When I heave myself back, I see my teenage self, a mournful devastated girl. I glimpse her, sitting in the nondescript suburban offices of Catholic Family Services, just outside Boston, not far from the Atlantic. She has been dis-embabied, this girl, a made up word that describes perfectly her condition. Now, though, sitting there in plain sight, she has hidden herself away. She thinks about escape, about morphing into a spirit able to fly through the window, and out into the clouds and over the blue Atlantic.

She sits between two older women, one of them her mother (*her motherless mother who did not know how to be a mother and refused to become a grandmother*) and the other a self-assured professional social worker, the one who'd never become a mother, who coaxed and cajoled her throughout her pregnancy, who'd convinced her, as they are themselves convinced (based on nothing but received ideas, ideas they've transformed into facts) that her son would be better off without her. That she would soon forget him and go on with her life.

Even in my imagination, I get stuck here, in that office with these two women. I can't understand how or why they do what they do. They don't know themselves. They are the carriers of their generation's religious and cultural beliefs. They may even be acting in good faith, but (perhaps without knowing) they are also interfering with history, with genetics, in a way that will carry through many generations. They congratulate themselves for what they are accomplishing, their own goodness, some kind of salvation for somebody, somewhere, but not for the girl who sits between them. She picks up the pen, signs her name, and represses all memory of the experience until she herself, becomes a grandmother.

Coda

The banshees of the Baby Scoop haunt long after the Baby Scoop has collapsed into the dust-bin of history. Changelings, shape-shifters, they are seen as pillars of the community: therapists and social workers and physicians and priests and nuns and ministers. They're do-gooders with many motivations, swollen with pride in their own goodness, their certainty that their power comes to them straight from God.

They gather around you, these ancients with what looks like, and sounds like, ancient wisdom, their determination, their power. They surround you, you who have no power, not even over your own body.

Long after their work is complete, after they've gotten what they're after (your baby), they abide in the shadows of your mind and heart, singing and spinning. They never stop. For the rest of your life, you see them and hear them in your dreams and in your waking thoughts. They repeat each other's lines, echo the same litanies, prayers, choruses, ejaculations. You hear them as you fall asleep and as you wake up in the morning. You hear them in your night dreams and your daydreams. You cannot get them out of your head.

They tell you:

You're bad. So bad

Your baby will be better off without you

You are irresponsible
Immature
A wild crazy girl
A sinner
A Slut
Depraved, not to mention delinquent
No good
No damned good!

If you really love your baby you will surrender him or her or them. You will give him/her/them to someone superior in every possible way to yourself

If you really love your baby you will relinquish him or her or them so that he or she or they will not be tainted by having you, its mistake mother, in his or her or their life

You will forget how they snatched the baby from your body the moment he emerged from it

Your experience will become a blur, distant, a small spot back in the depths of your memory, a tiny bat clinging to the roof of a vast deep cave, impossible to reach. You'll forget. You'll go on with your life as if this never happened.

Acknowledgements

I want to thank the estimable Steve Almond – writer, teacher, provocateur – for teaching me, in numerous workshops and tutorials over the course of several years, the writing strategies that were crucial to developing of this memoir: how to write about the hardest things, and how slow down where it hurts.

I would also like to thank Joshua D. Fischer – writer, editor, musician, all-around mensch – for his steadfast support during the writing of this book, and particularly with developing the book design and eyes on the final manuscript.

And finally Sarah P. Burns, birth mother, advocate and activist, who took me by the hand at the CUB Retreat in 2018 to show me a way out of the fog.

About the Author

Julia MacDonnell's long and varied writing career includes journalism and essays; book reviews; a short story collection and two novels. She received a 2024 individual artist fellowship from the New Jersey State Council on the Arts. Her 2021 story collection, **The Topography of Hidden Stories**, won the 2022 Next Generation Indie Book Award. The author and critic Joan Mellen called it, "a triumph of imaginative grace worthy of Alice Munro. " Her second novel, **Mimi Malloy, At Last!**, published by Picador in 2014, was chosen as an 'Indie Next' selection by the ABA. *People Magazine* called it, "Cathartic, suspenseful and droll...Mimi offers a hopeful take on both old age and bad blood." Her first novel, **A Year of Favor,** based loosely on the murders of four churchwomen in El Salvador in 1979, was published in 1994 by William Morrow & Co. Kirkus praised it as "Powerful first fiction...A convincing evocation of life in a Central American country...and a compelling portrait of a gusty, post-feminist heroine."

MacDonnell is professor emeritus in the Writing Arts department at Rowan University in Glassboro, New Jersey where she taught undergraduate and graduate writing classes for over twenty years, and developed the creative writing curriculum for its Master of Arts in Writing program. She is a former nonfiction editor of *Philadelphia Stories*. Now a grandmother of three, she lives in Maplewood, New Jersey, a couple of miles from her daughter Suzanne's family.

Selected Bibliography

Wake Up Little Susie: Single Pregnancy and Race before Roe v. Wade
Rickie Solinger
Routledge, 2000

Fallen Women, Problem Girls: Unmarried Mothers and the
Professionalization of Social Work, 1890-1945
Regina G. Kunzel
Yale University Press, 1993
Pulp Fictions and Problem Girls: Reading and Rewriting Single
Pregnancy in the Postwar United States
American Historical Review, 1995

The Girls Who Went Away: The Hidden History of Women Who
Surrendered Children for Adoption in the Decades Before Roe v. Wade
Ann Fessler
Penquin 2007

Helping Unmarried Mothers
Rose Bernstein
Association Press, 1971

The Primal Wound: Understanding the Adopted Child
Nancy Verrier
Gateway Press, 1993

The Baby Scoop Era: Unwed Mothers, Infant Adoption, Forced Surrender
Karen Wilson-Buterbaugh
Self-published, 2017

Journey of the Adopted Self, a Quest for Wholeness
Betty Jean Lifton
Basic Books, 1994

Twice Born, Memoirs of an Adopted Daughter
McGraw-Hill, 1975

Lost and Found, the Adoption Experience
University of Michigan Press, 2009

Shared Fate: A Theory ad Method of Adoptive Relationships
H. David Kirk
Ben-Simon Pubns, 1984

Recommended Readings

Relinquished: The Politics of Adoption and the Privilege of
American Motherhood
Gretchen Sisson
2024, St. Martin's Press

American Baby: A Mother, A Child and the Shadow History of Adoption
Gabrielle Glaser
Viking, 2021

All You Can Ever Know
Nicole Chung
Catapult, 2019

I Would Meet You Anywhere
Susan Kiyo Ito
The Ohio University Press, 2024

Following the Tambourine Man: A Birth Mother's Memoir
Janet Mason Ellerby
University of Syracuse Press, 2007

I'll Always Carry You: A Mother's Story of Adoption Loss, Grief,
and Healing
Linda L. Franklin
Authority Publishing, 2019

Goodbye Again,
Candace Cahill
Legacy Press, 2022

Surrender: A Memoir of Nature, Nurture and Love
Marylee MacDonald
Grand Canyon Press, 2020

You'll Forget All This Ever Happened: Secrets, Shame, and Adoption in the 1960s
Laura Engel
She Writes Press, 2022

I Knew You Were There: A Stolen Child's Search for her Irish Mother
Marie O'Leary Wydra and Megan Wydra McKercher
Shannon Press, 2022

Writing as a Way of Healing
Louise DeSalvo
Beacon Press, 1999